The Support Guide to Football League Clubs 1993

CW00482702

EDITOR
John Robinson

Ninth Edition

CONTENTS

British Library Cataloguing in Publication Data
The Supporters' Guide to Football League Clubs - 9th Edition
1. Great Britain. Football League Football Clubs - Robinson, editor
I. Robinson, John 1947
796 334 '63' 02541
ISBN 0-947808-20-5

Copyright © 1992; SOCCER BOOK PUBLISHING LTD. (0472-696226)
72, St. Peters' Avenue, Cleethorpes, Sth. Humberside, DN35 8HU, England

Printed by Adlard Print & Typesetting Services, The Old School, The Green, Ruddington, Notts. NG11 6HH

FOREWORD

The 'Super' League has now arrived and, no doubt to avoid breaching the Trade Descriptions Act, it is to be called 'The Premier League'. Supporters could be forgiven for thinking that the only change is the name!

As usual, therefore, Football faces an uncertain future (I have made this point, for one reason or another, every year since 1982!), but I am sure that it will pull through without too much difficulty.

Attendances, incidentally, were up by almost one million during the season although the average attendances for 1st & 2nd Division clubs were slightly down:

DIVISION	Nº games 1991/92	Nº games 1990/91	1991/92 TOTAL	1991/92 AVE	1990/91 TOTAL	1990/91 AVE
1st	462	381	10,009,385	21,665	8,607,532	22,591
2nd	552	552	5,799,247	10,506	6,278,508	11,374
3rd	552	552	2,981,918	5,402	2,836,523	5,138
4th	462	552	1,604,286	3,472	1,776,598	3,218
TOTALS	2,028	2,037	20,392,836	10,057	19,499,161	9,572

We are indebted to the staffs of the clubs featured in this guide for their cooperation and also to Michael Robinson (page layouts), Darren Kirk (cover artwork), Chris Ambler (photos), and David Collins and Malcolm Stammers for Welsh Information.

We are delighted to be able to include an extensive new section for disabled supporters and thank Jeremy Driscoll for his advice about the range of information to be included in this section. Other new sections include 1991/92 results and tables and additional admission information and readers should note that because so many grounds are in the course of redevelopment, capacities, family and away sections may change.

Supporters of Non-League and Scottish League clubs should note that we now publish THE SUPPORTERS' GUIDE TO NON-LEAGUE FOOTBALL CLUBS (£4.99) and THE SUPPORTERS' GUIDE TO SCOTTISH FOOTBALL (£3.99) both of which are available, post free, from the address opposite.

Finally, we would like to wish our readers a happy and safe spectating season.

John Robinson
EDITOR

WELSH NATIONAL STADIUM

Re-Opened for Football: 31st May 1989	**Pitch Size**: 110 × 69yds
Location: Cardiff City Centre, CARDIFF	**Ground Capacity**: 51,374
Telephone: (0222) 390111 (Ground)	**Seating Capacity**: 42,355
Telephone: (0222) 372325 (F.A. of Wales)	(40,240 for Football Matches)
Address: The National Ground, Cardiff Arms Park, Westgate Street, CARDIFF, Wales	

GENERAL INFORMATION
Car Parking: City Centre Car Parks
Coach Parking: By Police Direction
Nearest Railway Station: 5-10 minutes walk
Nearest Bus Station: 5 minutes walk
Nearest Police Station: Cardiff Centre
Police Force: South Wales
Police Telephone No.: (0222) 222111

GROUND INFORMATION
Family Facilities: Location of Stand:
Lower Tier of North & South Stands
Capacity of Stand: Not Specified

DISABLED SUPPORTERS INFORMATION
Wheelchairs: Accommodated in Disabled Section - North Side of West Stand - space for 24 wheelchairs
Disabled Toilets: Yes

ADMISSION INFO (1992/93 PRICES)
Adult Seating: £6.00 - £20.00
Child Seating: Half-price in Family Enclosures
Programme Price: £2.00
FAX Number: (0222) 343961
Note: Prices vary depending on the opponents & type of game.

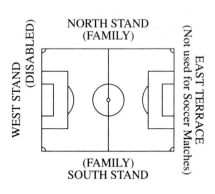

Travelling Supporters Information:
Routes: Exit M4 at Junction 29 and take A48(M) following signs for Cardiff City Centre (via A470). Use City Centre Public Car Parks.
From Cardiff Central Railway Station proceed past Bus Station, cross Wood Street and turn down Westgate Street (alongside the back of the Royal Hotel).

WEMBLEY STADIUM

Opened: 1923	**Ground Capacity**: 80,000
Location: Wembley, Middlesex HA9 0DW	**Seating Capacity**: 80,000
Telephone: Box Office (081) 900-1234	**Record Attendance**: 100,000
Telephone: Administration (081) 902-8833	**Pitch Size**: 115 × 75yds

GENERAL INFORMATION

Guided Tours Available: Telephone (081) 902-8833
Parking: Car Park for over 7,000 vehicles
Telephone Number: (071) 226-1627
Nearest Railway Stations: Wembley Park, Wembley Central, Wembley Complex (5-10 minutes walk)
Nearest Police Station: Mobile Unit in front of Twin Towers
Police Force Responsible for Crowd Control: Metropolitan
Police Telephone No.: (081) 900-7212

GROUND INFORMATION

All Sections of the Ground are Covered
Family Facilities: Location of Stand:
Family Enclosure, North Stand

DISABLED SUPPORTERS INFORMATION

Wheelchairs: Limited Facilities Available
Disabled Toilets: Yes
The Blind: No Special Facilities

ADMISSION INFO (1992/93 PRICES)

Admission £10.00 - £48.00; depending on the game and ground position. Also a £1 per seat booking fee

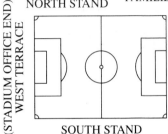

OLYMPIC WAY & TWIN TOWERS
(ROYAL BOX SIDE) FAMILIES
NORTH STAND
(STADIUM OFFICE END) WEST TERRACE
(PLAYERS TUNNEL END) EAST TERRACE
SOUTH STAND

HAMPDEN STADIUM

Opened: 1903
Location: In the 'Mount Florida' area of Glasgow, South East of the River Clyde
Telephone: Administration (041) 632-1275
Address: Hampden Park, Mount Florida, Glasgow   G42 9BA

Ground Capacity: 60,000   (To be changed - see Note)
Seating Capacity: 16,000
Record Attendance: 150,239
(Scotland vs. England 17/4/37)
Pitch Size: 115 × 75yds

GENERAL INFORMATION
Car Parking: Car Park for 1,200 vehicles
Coach Parking: Stadium Car Park
Nearest Railway Station: Mount Florida & Kings Park (both 5 minutes walk)
Nearest Police Station: Aikenhead Road, Glasgow G1?
Police Force Responsible for Crowd Control: Strathclyde
Police Telephone No.: (041) 422-1113

GROUND INFORMATION
Family Facilities: **Location of Stand**:
Varies from game to game
Capacity of Stand: -

DISABLED SUPPORTERS INFORMATION
Wheelchairs: Accommodated in Disabled Spectators Terrace: 54 Wheelchairs, 48 Ambulance Seated, 120 Ambulance Standing
Disabled Toilets: Yes, by Disabled Area
The Blind: Personal Commentaries from the 'Blind Companions'
Note: The Stadium is in the course of redevelopment and 1992/93 Internationals will be played at Ibrox. However, the Skol Cup Final will be staged at the Stadium.

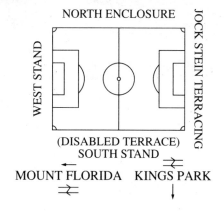

Travelling Supporters Information:
Routes: From the South: Take the A724 to the Cambuslang Road and at Eastfield branch left into Main Street and follow through Burnhill Street and Westmuir Place into Prospecthill Road. Turn left into Aikenhead Road and right into Mount Annan for Kinghorn Drive and the Stadium; From the South: Take the A77 Fenwick Road, through Kilmarnock Road into Pollokshaws Road then turn right into Langside Avenue. Pass through Battle Place to Battlefield Road and turn left into Cathcart Road. Turn right into Letherby Drive, right into Carmunnock Road and 1st left into Mount Annan Drive for the Stadium; From the North & East: Exit M8 Junction 15 and passing Infirmary on left proceed into High Street and cross the Albert Bridge into Crown Street. Join Cathcart Road and proceed South to the end then turn left and left again into Mount Annan Drive.

ARSENAL FC

Founded: 1886	**Record Attendance**: 73,295 (9/3/35)
Turned Professional: 1891	**Colours**: Shirts - Red with White Sleeves
Limited Company: 1893	Shorts - White
Admitted to League: 1893	**Telephone No.**: (071) 226-0304
Former Name(s): Royal Arsenal (1886-91);	**Ticket Information**: (071) 359-0131
Woolwich Arsenal (1891-1914)	**Pitch Size**: 110 × 71yds
Nickname: 'Gunners'	**Ground Capacity**: 41,188
Ground: Arsenal Stadium, Avenell Road,	**Seating Capacity**: 18,140
Highbury, London N5 1BU	

GENERAL INFORMATION

Supporters Club Administrator: Barry Baker
Address: 154 St.Thomas's Road, Finsbury Park, London   N4
Telephone Number: (071) 226-1627
Car Parking: Street Parking
Coach Parking: Drayton Park (N5)
Nearest Railway Station: Drayton Park/ Finsbury Park
Nearest Tube Station: Arsenal (Piccadilly) Adjacent
Club Shop:
Opening Times: Weekdays 9.30-5.00 Sat. Matchdays 1.00pm onwards
Telephone No.: (071) 226-9562
Postal Sales: Yes
Nearest Police Station: 284 Hornsey Road, Holloway
Police Force: Metropolitan
Police Telephone No.: (071) 263-9090

GROUND INFORMATION

Away Supporters' Entrances: Highbury Hill Turnstiles
Away Supporters' Sections: South Terrace   (Clock End) - Partially covered
Family Facilities: **Location of Stand**: North Side of West Stand
Capacity of Stand: 800

ADMISSION INFO (1992/93 PRICES)

Adult Standing: £8.00
Adult Seating: £10.50 - £22.00
Child Standing: £4.00
Child Seating: £5.00 (members only)
Programme Price: £1.50
FAX Number: (071) 226-0329

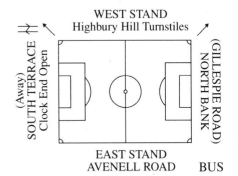

Travelling Supporters Information:
Routes: From North: Exit M1 junction 2 following City signs. After Holloway Road Station (6.25 miles) 3rd left into Drayton Park, after 0.75 mile right into Aubert Park and 2nd left into Avenell Road. From South:From London Bridge follow signs to Bank of England then Angel. Right at Traffic-lights to Highbury Roundabout (1 mile), into Holloway Road then 3rd right into Drayton Park (then as North). From West: Exit M4 Junction 1 towards Chiswick (A315), left after 1 mile (A40) to M41 the A40(M) to A501 Ring Road turn left at Angel to Highbury Roundabout (then as South).

ASTON VILLA FC

Founded: 1874	**Record Attendance**: 76,588 (2/3/46)
Turned Professional: 1885	**Colours**: Shirts - Claret with Blue Sleeves
Limited Company: 1896	Shorts - White
Admitted to League: 1888 (Founder)	**Telephone No.**: (021) 327-2299
Former Name(s): None	**Ticket Information**: (021) 327-5353
Nickname: 'The Villans'; 'Villa'	**Pitch Size**: 115 × 75yds
Ground: Villa Park, Trinity Road,	**Ground Capacity**: 40,312
Birmingham B6 6HE	**Seating Capacity**: 20,281

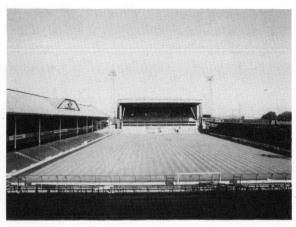

GENERAL INFORMATION

Supporters Club Administrator: -
Address: c/o Club's Commercial Dept.
Telephone Number: (021) 327-5399
Car Parking: Asda Car Park, Aston Hall Rd.
Coach Parking: Asda Car Park
Nearest Railway Station: Witton
Nearest Bus Station: Birmingham Centre
Club Shop:
Opening Times: Weekdays/Matchdays
9.30-5.00 (Closes for Match)
Telephone No.: (021) 327-2800
Postal Sales: Yes
Nearest Police Station: Queen's Road,
Aston (0.5 mile)
Police Force: West Midlands
Police Telephone No.: (021) 322-6010

GROUND INFORMATION

Away Supporters' Entrances: All Seating - Doors P,
Q & R
Away Supporters' Sections: Witton Lane Stand (P &
Q) and Witton End. Seating in both
Family Facilities: **Location of Stand**:
North Stand
Capacity of Stand: 3,940

ADMISSION INFO (1992/93 PRICES)

Adult Standing: £9.00
Adult Seating: £10.00 or £12.00 (Away fans £11.00)
Child Standing: £5.00
Child Seating: £5.00 or £6.00
Programme Price: £1.00
FAX Number: (021) 322-2107

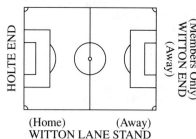

Travelling Supporters Information:
Routes: From all parts: Exit M6 Junction 6 (Spaghetti Junction). Follow signs Birmingham (NE). 3rd Exit
at Roundabout and in 0.5 mile, right into Aston Hall Road.
Bus Services: Service 7 from Corporation Street to Witton Square, also specials.

BARNET FC

Founded: 1888
Turned Professional: 1891
Limited Company: 1893
Admitted to League: 1991
Former Name(s): Barnet Alston
Nickname: 'Bees'
Ground: Underhill Stadium, Barnet Lane, Barnet, Herts. EN5 2BE

Record Attendance: 11,026 (1952)
Colours: Shirts - Amber
Shorts - Black
Telephone No.: (081) 441-6932
Ticket Information: (081) 449-4173
Pitch Size: 113 × 72yds
Ground Capacity: 9,786
Seating Capacity: 1,000

GENERAL INFORMATION
Supporters Club Administrator: Liz Ashfield
Address: 42 Connaught Road, Barnet, Herts.
Telephone Number: (081) 440-6625
Car Parking: Street Parking/ High Barnet Underground Car park
Coach Parking: By Police Direction
Nearest Railway Station: New Barnet (1.5 miles)
Nearest Tube Station: High Barnet (Northern) 5 mins.
Club Shop:
Opening Times: Wednesdays 10.00-4.00pm & Matchdays opens 2 hours before kick-off
Telephone No.: (081) 364-9601
Postal Sales: Yes
Nearest Police Station: Barnet (0.25 mile)
Police Force: Metropolitan
Police Telephone No.: (081) 200-2212

GROUND INFORMATION
Away Supporters' Entrances: Priory Grove
Away Supporters' Sections: East Terrace
Family Facilities: **Location of Stand**: Barnet Lane
Capacity of Stand: 200

ADMISSION INFO (1992/93 PRICES)
Adult Standing: £6.00
Adult Seating: £10.00
Child Standing: £3.00
Child Seating: £10.00
Programme Price: £1.00
FAX Number: (081) 447-0655

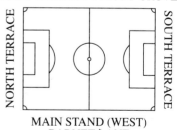

EAST TERRACE   PRIORY GROVE

NORTH TERRACE

SOUTH TERRACE

MAIN STAND (WEST)
BARNET LANE

Travelling Supporters Information:
Routes: The ground is situated off the Great North Road (A1000) at the foot of Barnet Hill near to the junction with Station Road (A110). Barnet Lane is on to the West of the A1000 next to the Cricket ground.

BARNSLEY FC

Founded: 1887	**Record Attendance**: 40,255 (15/2/36)
Turned Professional: 1888	**Colours**: Shirts - Red
Limited Company: 1899	Shorts - White
Admitted to League: 1898	**Telephone No.**: (0226) 295353
Former Name(s): Barnsley St.Peter's	**Ticket Information**: (0226) 295353
Nickname: 'Tykes'; 'Colliers'; 'Reds'	**Pitch Size**: 110 × 75yds
Ground: Oakwell Ground, Grove Street,	**Ground Capacity**: 26,586
Barnsley, S71 1ET	**Seating Capacity**: 2,154

GENERAL INFORMATION
Supporters Club Administrator: Mr.S.Curry
Address: c/o Barnsley F.C. Social Club, Oakwell Ground, Barnsley
Telephone Number: (0226) 287664
Car Parking: Queen's Ground Car Park (adjacent)
Coach Parking: Queen's Ground Car Park
Nearest Railway Station: Barnsley Exchange
Nearest Bus Station: Barnsley
Club Shop:
Opening Times: Weekdays 9.00-5.00 Saturday Matchdays 9.00-5.30; Saturdays with no home Matches 9.00-12.00
Telephone No.: (0226) 295353
Postal Sales: Yes
Nearest Police Station: Churchfields, Barnsley
Police Force: South Yorkshire
Police Telephone No.: (0226) 206161

GROUND INFORMATION
Away Supporters' Entrances: Spion Kop Turnstiles (Numbers 41 to 47)
Away Supporters' Sections: Spion Kop
Family Facilities:
Accommodated throughout the Ground

ADMISSION INFO (1992/93 PRICES)
Adult Standing: £5.50 or £6.00
Adult Seating: £10.00
Child Standing: £4.00
Child Seating: £5.00 (Only if purchased before matchday. Otherwise £10.00)
Programme Price: £1.00
FAX Number: (0226) 201000

BREWERY STAND

SPION KOP (Away)

PONTEFRACT ROAD END

DISABLED STAND   MAIN STAND

Travelling Supporters Information:
Routes: From All Parts: Exit M1 Junction 37 and follow 'Football Ground' signs to ground (2 miles).

BIRMINGHAM CITY FC

Founded: 1875
Turned Professional: 1885
Limited Company: 1888
Admitted to League: 1892
Former Name(s): Small Heath Alliance FC
(187-88); Small Heath FC (1888-1905);
Birmingham FC (1905-1945)
Nickname: 'Blues'
Ground: St. Andrew's, St. Andrew's Street,
Birmingham B9 4NH

Record Attendance: 68,844 (11/2/39)
Colours: Shirts - Blue and White
Shorts - White
Telephone No.: (021) 772-0101/2689
Ticket Information: (021) 766-8274
Pitch Size: 115 × 75yds
Ground Capacity: 28,235
Seating Capacity: 8,868

GENERAL INFORMATION
Supp. Club Administrator: Linda Godman
Address: 69 Malmesbury Road, Small Heath, Birmingham
Telephone Number: (021) 773-5088
Car Parking: Coventry Road & Cattell Road Car Parks
Coach Parking: Tilton Road
Nearest Railway Station: Birmingham New Street
Nearest Bus Station: Digbeth
Club Shop:
Opening Times: Weekdays 9.30-4.30
Saturday Matchdays 9.30-6.00
Telephone No.: (021) 766-8274
Postal Sales: Yes
Nearest Police Station: Bordesley Green (0.5 mile)
Police Force: West Midlands
Police Telephone No.: (021) 772-1166

GROUND INFORMATION
Away Supporters' Entrances: Entrance 'J' Tilton Rd.
Away Supporters' Sections: Tilton Road End
Family Facilities: Location of Stand:
City End
Capacity of Stand: 2,343

ADMISSION INFO (1992/93 PRICES)
Adult Standing: £6.50
Adult Seating: £8.00 - £10.00
Child Standing: £4.00
Child Seating: £5.00
Programme Price: £1.00
FAX Number: (021) 766-7866

CATTELL ROAD STAND

TILTON ROAD END (Away)

EMMELINE STREET (RAILWAY END) CITY END

CITY END

ST. ANDREW'S STREET STAND

REMPLOY ENCLOSURE

Travelling Supporters Information:
Routes: From All Parts: Exit M6 Junction 6, to A38(M) (Aston Expressway), leave at 2nd exit then 1st exit at Roundabout along Dartmouth Middleway, after 1.25 miles take left into St. Andrew's Street.
Bus Services: Service 97 from Birmingham: Services 98 & 99 from Digbeth.

BLACKBURN ROVERS FC

Founded: 1875
Turned Professional: 1880
Limited Company: 1897
Admitted to League: 1888 (Founder)
Former Name(s): Blackburn Grammar
School Old Boys FC
Nickname: 'Rovers'; 'Blues & Whites'
Ground: Ewood Park, Blackburn,
Lancashire, BB2 4JF

Record Attendance: 61,783 (2/3/29)
Colours: Shirts - Blue & White Halves
Shorts - White
Telephone No.: (0254) 55432
Ticket Information: (0254) 55432
Pitch Size: 117 × 73yds
Ground Capacity: 15,147
Seating Capacity: 7,062

GENERAL INFORMATION
Supporters Club Administrator:
Barbara Magee
Address: c/o Club
Telephone Number: (0254) 55432
Car Parking: Street Parking (nearby)
Coach Parking: By Police direction
Nearest Railway Station: Blackburn
Central (1.5 miles)
Nearest Bus Station: Blackburn Central
(1.5 miles)
Club Shop:
Opening Times: Weekdays 9.00-5.00
Saturday Matchdays 9.30-5.00
Telephone No.: (0254) 55432
Postal Sales: Yes
Nearest Police Station: Blackburn (2 miles)
Police Force: Lancashire
Police Telephone No.: (0254) 51212

GROUND INFORMATION
Blackburn F.C. regret that no accommodation will
be available to Visitors during the 1992-1993 Season
due to re-development of the Darwen End.
Family Facilities: Location of Stand:
In Walkersteel Stand
Capacity of Stand: Approx. 629

ADMISSION INFO (1992/93 PRICES)
Adult Standing: £7.00
Adult Seating: £10.00 - £12.00
Child Standing: £7.00
Child Seating: £6.00 - £8.00
Programme Price: £1.00
FAX Number: (0254) 671042

(MEMBERS ONLY)
RIVERSIDE LANE
WALKERSTEEL STAND

← HOME SUPPORTERS ONLY
KIDDER STREET
BLACKBURN END

CLOSED FOR RE-DEVELOPMENT
DARWEN END

NUTTALL STREET STAND
BOLTON ROAD
(MEMBERS ONLY)

Travelling Supporters Information:
Routes: From North, South and West: Exit M6 Junction 31, or take A666, follow signs for Blackburn then
for Bolton Road, after 1.5 miles turn left into Kidder Street.; From East: Use A679 or A677 and follow signs
for Bolton Road (then as above).

BLACKPOOL FC

Founded: 1887	**Record Attendance**: 38,098 (17/9/55)
Turned Professional: 1887	**Colours**: Shirts - Tangerine
Limited Company: 1896	Shorts - White
Admitted to League: 1896	**Telephone No.**: (0253) 404331
Former Name(s): Merged with Blackpool	**Ticket Information**: (0253) 404331
St.Johns 1887	**Pitch Size**: 111 × 73yds
Nickname: 'Seasiders'	**Ground Capacity**: 10,041
Ground: Bloomfield Road, Blackpool	**Seating Capacity**: 3,196
Lancashire, FY1 6JJ	

GENERAL INFORMATION

Supporters Club Administrator: J. Bentley
Address: Blackpool Supporters' Club, Bloomfield Road, Blackpool
Telephone Number: (0253) 46428 (evenings only 7pm-11pm)
Car Parking: Car Park at Ground (3,000 cars) and Street Parking
Coach Parking: Mecca Car Park (behind Spion Kop)
Nearest Railway Station: Blackpool South (5 minutes walk)
Nearest Bus Station: Talbot Road (2 miles)
Club Shop:
Opening Times: Daily 9.00-5.30
Telephone No.: (0253) 404331
Postal Sales: Yes
Nearest Police Station: South Shore, Waterloo Road, Blackpool
Police Force: Lancashire
Police Telephone No.: (0253) 293933

GROUND INFORMATION

Away Supporters' Entrances: Spion Kop Turnstiles
Away Supporters' Sections: Spion Kop (Open) & East Paddock North Section (Covered)
Family Facilities: **Location of Stand**: West Stand (South End)
Capacity of Stand: 400 (Family area)

ADMISSION INFO (1992/93 PRICES)

Adult Standing: £6.00
Adult Seating: £7.50
Child Standing: £4.00
Child Seating: £5.50
Programme Price: £1.00
FAX Number: (0253) 405011

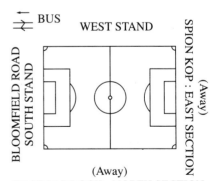

Travelling Supporters Information:

Routes: From All Parts: Exit M6 Junction 32 to M55. Follow signs for main car parks along new 'spine' road to car parks at side of ground.

BOLTON WANDERERS FC

Founded: 1874
Turned Professional: 1880
Limited Company: 1895
Admitted to League: 1888 (Founder)
Former Name(s): Christchurch FC (1874-77)
Nickname: 'Trotters'
Ground: Burnden Park, Manchester Road, Bolton   BL3 2QR

Record Attendance: 69,912 (18/2/33)
Colours: Shirts - White
                     Shorts - Blue
Telephone No.: (0204) 389200
Ticket Information: (0204) 21101
Pitch Size: 113 × 75yds
Ground Capacity: 22,772
Seating Capacity: 8,000

GENERAL INFORMATION
Supporters Club Administrator: None
Address: -
Telephone Number: -
Car Parking: Rosehill Car Park (Nearby)
Coach Parking: Rosehill Car Park Manchester Road
Nearest Railway Station: Bolton Trinity Street (0.5 mile)
Nearest Bus Station: Moor Lane, Bolton
Club Shop:
Opening Times: Daily 9.30-5.30
Telephone No.: (0204) 389200
Postal Sales: Yes
Nearest Police Station: Howell Croft; Bolton
Police Force: Greater Manchester
Police Telephone No.: (0204) 22466

GROUND INFORMATION
Away Supporters' Entrances: Embankment Turnstiles
Away Supporters' Sections: Embankment (Open) & Covered Seating
Family Facilities: Location of Stand: Greater Lever Stand
Capacity of Stand: 3,000

ADMISSION INFO (1992/93 PRICES)
Adult Standing: £7.00
Adult Seating: £7.00 - £9.00
Child Standing: £4.50
Child Seating: £4.50 - £5.50
Programme Price: £1.00
FAX Number: (0204) 382334

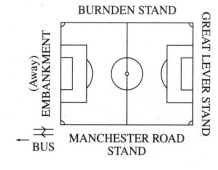

Travelling Supporters Information:
Routes: From North: Exit M61 Junction 5 or use A666 or A676. Follow signs for Farnworth (B653) into Manchester Road. After 0.5 mile turn left into Croft Lane; From South, East and West: Exit M62 Junction 14 to M61, after 2 miles leave motorway then 1st exit at Roundabout (B6536). After 2 miles turn right into Croft Lane.

AFC BOURNEMOUTH

Founded: 1890	**Record Attendance**: 28,799 (2/3/57)
Turned Professional: 1912	**Colours**: Shirts - Red and Black Stripes
Limited Company: 1914	Shorts - White
Admitted to League: 1923	**Telephone No.**: (0202) 395381
Former Name(s): Boscombe St.Johns FC	**Ticket Information**: (0202) 395381
(1890-99); Boscombe FC (1899-1923)	**Pitch Size**: 112 × 75yds
Bournemouth & Boscombe Ath. FC (1923-72)	**Ground Capacity**: 11,433
Nickname: 'Cherries'	**Seating Capacity**: 3,813
Ground: Dean Court, Bournemouth, Dorset	BH7 7AF

GENERAL INFORMATION

Supporters Club Administrator: -
Address: Dean Court Supporters' Club
Bournemouth BH7 7AF
Telephone Number: (0202) 398313
Car Parking: Car Park (1500 cars) Behind
Main Stand
Coach Parking: Kings Park (Nearby)
Nearest Railway Station: Bournemouth
Central (1.5 miles)
Nearest Bus Station: Holdenhurst Road,
Bournemouth
Club Shop:
Opening Times: Weekdays 9.30-5.30
Saturday Matchdays 9.30 to Kick-off
Closed on Wednesdays
Telephone No.: (0202) 303469
Postal Sales: Yes
Nearest Police Station: Boscombe (400 yds)
Police Force: Dorset
Police Telephone No.: (0202) 552099

GROUND INFORMATION

Away Supporters' Entrances: Main Stand Turnstiles
(Block A)
Away Supporters' Sections: Brighton Beach Terrace
(Open)
Family Facilities: Location of Stand:
Family Block (Main Stand)
Capacity of Stand: 700

ADMISSION INFO (1992/93 PRICES)

Adult Standing: £5.00
Adult Seating: £7.00 - £9.00
Child Standing: £3.00
Child Seating: £3.00
Programme Price: £1.00
FAX Number: (0202) 309797

Travelling Supporters Information:

Routes: From North & East: Take A338 into Bournemouth and turn left at 'Kings Park' turning. Then first left at mini-roundabout and first right into Thistlebarrow Road for Ground. From West: Use A3049, turning right at Wallisdown Roundabout to Talbot Roundabout. Take first exit at Talbot Roundabout (over Wessex Way), then left at mini-roundabout. Go straight across traffic lights then right at mini-roundabout into Kings Park for ground.
Bus Services: Service 25 passes ground.

BRADFORD CITY FC

Founded: 1903
Turned Professional: 1903
Limited Company: 1908 (Reformed 1983)
Admitted to League: 1903
Former Name(s): None
Nickname: 'Bantams'
Ground: Valley Parade, Bradford   BD8 7DY

Record Attendance: 39,146 (11/3/11)
Colours: Shirts - Claret & Amber
            Shorts - Claret
Telephone No.: (0274) 306062
Ticket Information: (0274) 307050
Pitch Size: 110 × 80yds
Ground Capacity: 14,810
Seating Capacity: 6,500

GENERAL INFORMATION

Supporters Club Administrator:
Mrs J. Calvert
Address: 1 Westmoor Avenue, Baildon
BD17 5HG
Telephone Number: (0274) 591947
Car Parking: Street Parking and car parks
(£2 entry charge)
Coach Parking: By Police direction
Nearest Railway Station: Bradford
Interchange
Nearest Bus Station: Bradford Interchange
Club Shop:
Opening Times: Monday to Saturday
10.00am-5.00pm
Telephone No.: (0274) 306062
Postal Sales: Yes
Nearest Police Station: Tyrrells, Bradford
Police Force: West Yorkshire
Police Telephone No.: (0274) 723422

GROUND INFORMATION

Away Supporters' Entrances: Midland Road
Away Supporters' Sections: Midland Road Side
Family Facilities: Location of Stand:
Charlie Brown's Family Stand
Capacity of Stand: 2,000 seated

ADMISSION INFO (1992/93 PRICES)

Adult Standing: £5.50
Adult Seating: £7.00 - £9.00
Child Standing: £3.00
Child Seating: £3.50 - £5.00
Programme Price: £1.00
FAX Number: (0274) 307457

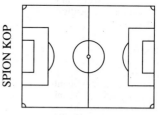

Travelling Supporters Information:

Routes: From North: Take A650 and follow signs for Bradford. A third of a mile after junction with Ring Road turn left into Valley Parade. From East, South and West: Take M62 and exit Junction 26 onto M606. At end take 2nd left from roundabout and onto A6177 Ring Road. At next roundabout (3rd exit) turn right to City Centre (A614). At second roundabout turn right onto Central Ring Road (A6181) then left at next roundabout and left again at following roundabout marked 'Local Access Only'. Pass through traffic lights at the top of the hill following Keighley (A650) sign. Ground is then 0.5 mile along on the right.

BRENTFORD FC

Founded: 1889	**Record Attendance**: 39,626 (5/3/38)
Turned Professional: 1899	**Colours**: Shirts - Red and White Stripes
Limited Company: 1901	Shorts - Black
Admitted to League: 1920	**Telephone No.**: (081) 847-2511
Former Name(s): None	**Ticket Information**: (081) 847-2511
Nickname: 'Bees'	**Pitch Size**: 110 × 73yds
Ground: Griffin Park, Braemar Road,	**Ground Capacity**: 12,452
Brentford, Middlesex TW8 0NT	**Seating Capacity**: 4,000

GENERAL INFORMATION
Supporters Club Administrator:
Mr. P. Gilham
Address: 16 Hartland Road, Hampton Hill
Middlesex
Telephone Number: (081) 941-0425
Car Parking: Street Parking
Coach Parking: Layton Road Car Park
Nearest Railway Station: Brentford Central
Nearest Tube Station: South Ealing
(Piccadilly)
Club Shop:
Opening Times: Monday-Friday &
Matchdays 10.00-4.00
Telephone No.: (081) 560-9856
Postal Sales: Yes
Nearest Police Station: Brentford
Police Force: Metropolitan
Police Telephone No.: (081) 569-9728

GROUND INFORMATION
Away Supporters' Entrances: Ealing Road Turnstiles
Away Supporters' Sections: Ealing Road End (Open)
- Covered accommodation in wet weather
Family Facilities: **Location of Stand**:
Brook Road End
Capacity of Stand: 600

ADMISSION INFO (1992/93 PRICES)
Adult Standing: £5.50 Member   £7 Non-member
Adult Seating: £8 - £9 Member   £10 Non-member
Child Standing: £3.50 Member   £5 Non-member
Child Seating: £5 - £7 Member   £8 Non-member
Programme Price: £1.50
FAX Number: (081) 568-9940
(Seating Prices are 1991/92 Prices)

```
              NEW ROAD TERRACING
  SEATS & TERRACING                    EALING ROAD TERRACING
  BROOK ROAD

              MAIN STAND
  ← ⇄ BRAEMAR ROAD
        SEATS & TERRACING
```

Travelling Supporters Information:
Routes: From North & East: Take A406 North Circular (from M1/A1) to Chiswick. Follow South Circular signs for 0.25 mile then turn right A315. After 0.5 mile turn right into Ealing Road. From West: Exit M4 Junction 2, U-turn at lights (legal), take A4 heading West. In 0.5 mile turn left into Ealing Road. From South: Use A3/M3/A240 or A316 to Junction South Circular (A205) over Kew Bridge turn left on to A315 turn right (0.5 mile) into Ealing Road.

BRIGHTON & HOVE ALBION FC

Founded: 1900
Turned Professional: 1900
Limited Company: 1904
Admitted to League: 1920
Former Name(s): Brighton & Hove Rangers FC (1900-01)
Nickname: 'Seagulls'
Ground: Goldstone Ground, Old Shoreham Road, Hove, Sussex, BN3 7DE

Record Attendance: 36,747 (27/12/58)
Colours: Shirts - Blue & White Stripes
Shorts - Blue
Telephone No.: (0273) 739535
Ticket Information: (0273) 778855
Pitch Size: 112 × 75yds
Ground Capacity: 18,647
Seating Capacity: 5,274

GENERAL INFORMATION
Supporters Club Administrator: Liz Costa
Address: 72 Stoneham Road, Hove BN3 5HH
Telephone Number: (0273) 739535
Car Parking: Greyhound Stadium and street parking
Coach Parking: Conway Street, Hove
Nearest Railway Station: Hove (5 minutes walk)
Nearest Bus Station: Brighton Pool Valley
Club Shop: Sports Express, Newtown Road
Opening Times: Weekdays 9.00-5.00
Telephone No.: (0273) 26412
Postal Sales: Yes
Nearest Police Station: Hove (1 mile)
Police Force: Sussex
Police Telephone No.: (0273) 778922

GROUND INFORMATION
Away Supporters' Entrances: Goldstone Lane Turnstiles
Away Supporters' Sections: South East Corner (Open Terrace); South Stand (Seats)
Family Facilities: **Location of Stand**: South Stand - Entrance Newtown Road
Capacity of Stand: 1,500

ADMISSION INFO (1992/93 PRICES)
Adult Standing: £5 Members   £6 Non-Members
Adult Seating: £8.50; £11.00; £13.00; £15.00
Child Standing: £3.50 Members   £6 Non-Members
Child Seating: £8.50-£15.00   Family - £5.50
Programme Price: £1.20
FAX Number: (0273) 21095

GOLDSTONE LANE   (Away)
N.E. TERRACE   EAST TERRACE
OLD SHOREHAM ROAD
NORTH TERRACE
NEWTOWN ROAD
SOUTH STAND
WEST STAND
NEWTOWN ROAD

Travelling Supporters Information:
Routes: From North: Take A23, turn right 2 miles after Pyecombe follow Hove signs for 1mile, bear left into Nevill Road (A2023), then turn left at Crossroads (1 mile), into Old Shoreham Road. From East: Take A27 to Brighton then follow Worthing signs into Old Shoreham Road. From West: Take A27 straight into Old Shoreham Road.
Bus Services: Service 11 passes ground.

BRISTOL CITY FC

Founded: 1894
Turned Professional: 1897
Limited Company: 1897
Admitted to League: 1901
Former Name(s): Bristol South End FC
(1894-7)
Nickname: 'Robins'
Ground: Ashton Gate, Winterstoke Road,
Ashton Road, Bristol BS3 2EJ

Record Attendance: 43,335 (16/2/35)
Colours: Shirts - Red
Shorts - White
Telephone No.: (0272) 632812
Ticket Information: (0272) 632812
Pitch Size: 120 × 75yds
Ground Capacity: 25,271
Seating Capacity: 16,000

GENERAL INFORMATION
Supporters Club Administrator:
Mr.G.Williams
Address: c/o Club
Telephone Number: (0272) 665554
Car Parking: Street Parking
Coach Parking: Cannon's March
Nearest Railway Station: Bristol Temple
Meads (1.5 miles)
Nearest Bus Station: Bristol City Centre
Club Shop:
Opening Times: Weekdays 9.00-5.00
& Matchdays
Telephone No.: (0272) 632812
Postal Sales: Yes
Nearest Police Station: Kings Mead Lane
(2 miles) - Office at ground
Police Force: Avon/Somerset
Police Telephone No.: (0272) 277777

GROUND INFORMATION
Away Supporters' Entrances: Ashton Road -
Turnstiles 51-57
Away Supporters' Sections: Ashton Road - Open End
Family Facilities: Location of Stand:
Dolman Stand
Capacity of Stand: 4,741

ADMISSION INFO (1992/93 PRICES)
Adult Standing: £6.00
Adult Seating: £6.00 - £9.50
Child Standing: £4.00
Child Seating: £4.00 - £7.00
Programme Price: £1.00
FAX Number: (0272) 639574

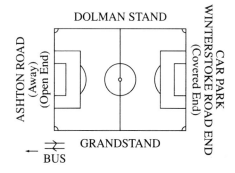

Travelling Supporters Information:
Routes: From North & West: Exit M5 Junction 16, take A38 to Bristol City Centre and follow A38 Taunton signs. Cross Swing Bridge (1.25 miles) and bear left into Winterstoke Road. From East: Take M4 then M32 follow signs to city centre (then as North & West). From South: Exit M5 Junction 18 and follow Taunton signs over Swing Bridge (then as above).
Bus Services: Service 51 from Railway Station.

BRISTOL ROVERS FC

Founded: 1883	**Record Attendance**: 18,000
Turned Professional: 1897	**Colours**: Shirts - Blue & White Quarters
Limited Company: 1896	Shorts - White
Admitted to League: 1920	**Telephone No.**: (0272) 352508
Former Name(s): Black Arabs FC (1883-84)	**Ticket Information**: (0272) 352508
Eastville Rovers FC (1884-96)	**Pitch Size**: 110 × 76yds
Bristol Eastville Rovers FC (1896-7)	**Ground Capacity**: 9,464
Nickname: 'Pirates'; 'Rovers'	**Seating Capacity**: 1,006
Ground: Twerton Park, Bath, Avon	**Office**: 199 Two Mile Hill Rd., Kingswood,
	Bristol BS15 7AZ

GENERAL INFORMATION

Supporters Club Administrator:
Mr. Steve Burns
Address: c/o Club's Office
Telephone Number: (0272) 510363
Car Parking: Very little space at ground
Coach Parking: Avon Street, Bath
Nearest Railway Station: Bath Spa
(1.5 miles)
Nearest Bus Station: Avon Street, Bath
Club Shop:
Opening Times: Weekdays (Club Offices)
9.00-5.00pm
Telephone No.: (0272) 352508
Postal Sales: Yes
Nearest Police Station: Bath (1.5 miles)
Police Force: Avon & Somerset
Police Telephone No.: (0225) 444343

GROUND INFORMATION

Away Supporters' Entrances: Turnstiles 20/21
Away Supporters' Sections: Bristol End
Family Facilities: **Location of Stand**:
Family Enclosure Terrace - Bath End
New Family Stand at side of Main Stand
Capacity of Stand: 236

ADMISSION INFO (1992/93 PRICES)

Adult Standing: £6.50
Adult Seating: £13.00 Main Stand   £9 Family Stand
Child Standing: £4.00
Child Seating: £8.50 Main Stand   £6 Family Stand
Away Fans: £6.50 - no concessions
Programme Price: £1.20
FAX Number: (0272) 353477

```
           HOME ENCLOSURE
             (COVERED)

 F                              B
 A                              R
 M                              I
 I                              S
 L                              T
 Y                              O
                                L
 E                              
 N                              E
 C                              N
 L                              D
 O                              
 S                            (Away)
 U                              
 R                              
 E                              
        Home   MEMBERS ENCLOSURE
      Turnstiles  MAIN STAND
        ←⇥
```

Travelling Supporters Information:
Routes: Take the A36 into Bath City Centre. Follow along Pulteney Road, then right into Claverton Street and along Lower Bristol Road (A36). Left under Railway (1.5 miles) into Twerton High Street and ground on left.

BURNLEY FC

Founded: 1882	**Record Attendance**: 54,775 (23/2/24)
Turned Professional: 1883	**Colours**: Shirts - Claret with Blue Sleeves
Limited Company: 1897	Shorts - White
Admitted to League: 1888 (Founder)	**Telephone No.**: (0282) 27777
Former Name(s): Burnley Rovers FC	**Ticket Information**: (0282) 27777
Nickname: 'Clarets'	**Pitch Size**: 115 × 73yds
Ground: Turf Moor, Brunshaw Road,	**Ground Capacity**: 20,912
Burnley, Lancs. BB10 4BX	**Seating Capacity**: 7,437

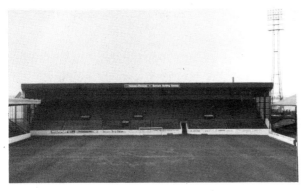

GENERAL INFORMATION
Supporters Club Administrator: David Spencer
Address: c/o Club
Telephone Number: (0282) 35176
Car Parking: Church Street & Fulledge Rec. Car Parks (5 minutes walk)
Coach Parking: By Police direction
Nearest Railway Station: Burnley Central (1.5 miles)
Nearest Bus Station: Burnley (5 mins. walk)
Club Shop:
Opening Times: Office Hours
Telephone No.: (0282) 27777
Postal Sales: Yes
Nearest Police Station: Parker Lane, Burnley (5 minutes walk)
Police Force: Lancashire
Police Telephone No.: (0282) 25001

GROUND INFORMATION
Away Supporters' Entrances: Belvedere Road Turnstiles
Away Supporters' Sections: Covered Terracing
Family Facilities: **Location of Stand**: Cricket Field Stand (Members Only)
Capacity of Stand: 4,276
Away Families: None

ADMISSION INFO (1992/93 PRICES)
Adult Standing: £6.00 or £6.50
Adult Seating: £6.00 - £10.00
Child Standing: £3.00
Child Seating: £3.50 - £5.00
Programme Price: £1.00
FAX Number: (0382) 28938

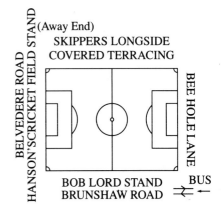

Travelling Supporters Information:
Routes: From North: Follow A56 to Town Centre and take 1st exit at roundabout into Yorkshire Street. Follow over crossroads into Brunshaw Road. From East: Follow A646 to A671 then along Todmorden Road to Town Centre. Follow down to crossroads and turn right into Brunshaw Road. From West & South: Exit M6 Junction 31, taking Blackburn bypass & A679 into Town Centre, take 3rd exit from roundabout into Yorkshire Street (then as North).

BURY FC

Founded: 1885	**Record Attendance**: 35,000 (9/1/60)
Turned Professional: 1885	**Colours**: Shirts - White
Limited Company: 1897	Shorts - Navy
Admitted to League: 1894	**Telephone No.**: (061) 764-4881
Former Name(s): None	**Ticket Information**: (061) 764-4881
Nickname: 'Shakers'	**Pitch Size**: 112×72yds
Ground: Gigg Lane, Bury, Lancs. BL9 9HR	**Ground Capacity**: 8,337
	Seating Capacity: 2,500

GENERAL INFORMATION
Supporters Club Administrator: P. Cullen
Address: c/o Club
Car Parking: Street Parking
Coach Parking: By Police Direction
Nearest Railway Station: Bury Interchange
(1 mile)
Nearest Bus Station: Bury Interchange
Club Shop:
Opening Times: Daily 9.00-5.00
Telephone No.: (061) 705-2144
Postal Sales: Yes (Price lists available)
Nearest Police Station: Irwell Street, Bury
Police Force: Greater Manchester
Police Telephone No.: (061) 872-5050

GROUND INFORMATION
Away Supporters' Entrances: Gigg Lane
Away Supporters' Sections: Cemetery End
Covered Terracing/ B.Stand Seating
Family Facilities: **Location of Stand**:
Family Stand - 'A' Stand
Capacity of Stand: 500

ADMISSION INFO (1992/93 PRICES)
Adult Standing: £7.00   (£5.50 Members)
Adult Seating: £7 - £9   (£5.50 - £7.50 Members)
Child Standing: £7.00   (£3.00 Members)
Child Seating: £5.50 - £7.50   (£3 - £4.50 Members)
Programme Price: £1.00
FAX Number: (061) 764-5521

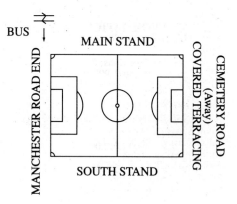

Travelling Supporters Information:
Routes: From North: Exit M66 Junction 2, take Bury Road (A58) for 0.5 mile, then turn left into Heywood Street and follow this into Parkhills Road until its end, turn left into Manchester Road (A56) then left into Gigg Lane. From South, East & West: Exit M62 Junction 17, take Bury Road (A56) for 3 miles then turn right into Gigg Lane.

CAMBRIDGE UNITED FC

Founded: 1919
Turned Professional: 1946
Limited Company: 1948
Admitted to League: 1970
Former Name(s): Abbey United FC (1919-49)
Nickname: 'U's'; 'United'
Ground: Abbey Stadium, Newmarket Road
Cambridge   CB5 8LL

Record Attendance: 14,000 (1/5/70)
Colours: Shirts - Amber
Shorts - Black
Telephone No.: (0223) 241237
Ticket Information: (0223) 241237
Pitch Size: 110 × 74yds
Ground Capacity: 10,100
Seating Capacity: 3,410

GENERAL INFORMATION
Supporters Club Administrator: -
Address: c/o Club
Telephone Number: -
Car Parking: Coldhams Common
Coach Parking: Coldhams Common
Nearest Railway Station: Cambridge (2mls)
Nearest Bus Station: Cambridge City Centre
Club Shop:
Opening Times: Weekdays 10.00-5.00
& Matchdays
Telephone No.: (0223) 241237
Postal Sales: Yes
Nearest Police Station:Parkside, Cambridge
Police Force: Cambridgeshire
Police Telephone No.: (0223) 358966

GROUND INFORMATION
Away Supporters' Entrances: Coldham Common
- Turnstiles 16-19
Away Supporters' Sections; South Terrace
(part covered - 360 seats/1,900 standing)
Family Facilities: Location of Stand:
Main Stand
Capacity of Stand: 200

ADMISSION INFO (1992/93 PRICES)
Adult Standing: £7.00
Adult Seating: £9.00 - £13.00
Child Standing: £3.00
Child Seating: £5.00 - £7.00
Programme Price: £1.00
FAX Number: (0223) 247874

ELFLEDA ROAD
MAIN STAND
Disabled

NEWMARKET ROAD
NORTH TERRACE

SOUTH TERRACE
(Away)

HABBIN STAND   Visitors
Entrance

Travelling Supporters Information:
Routes: From North: Take A1 and A604 into City Centre, then A45 Newmarket signs into Newmarket Road. From East: Take A45 straight into Newmarket Road. From South: Take A10 or A130 into City Centre (then as North). From West: Take A422 into Cambridge and pick up A45 into Newmarket Road.
Bus Services: Services 180 & 181 from Railway Station to City Centre/ 182 & 183 to Ground.

CARDIFF CITY FC

Founded: 1899	**Record Attendance**: 61,566 (14/10/61)
Turned Professional: 1910	**Colours**: Shirts - Blue
Limited Company: 1910	Shorts - White
Admitted to League: 1920	**Telephone No.**: (0222) 398636
Former Name(s): Riverside FC (1899-1910)	**Ticket Information**: (0222) 398636
Nickname: 'Bluebirds'	**Pitch Size**: 112 × 76yds
Ground: Ninian Park, Sloper Road,	**Ground Capacity**: 21,403
Cardiff, CF1 8SX	**Seating Capacity**: 5,563

GENERAL INFORMATION
Supporters Club Administrator:
Mr. M. Lambert
Address: 2 Station Villas, Llwyd-Coed,
Aberdare, Mid. Glamorgan
Telephone Number: (0685) 881006
Car Parking: Sloper Road & Street Parking
Coach Parking: Sloper Road (Adjacent)
Nearest Railway Station: Cardiff Central
(1 mile)
Nearest Bus Station: Cardiff Central
Club Shop:
Opening Times: Weekdays 9.00-5.00
& Matchdays 1.5 hours before kick-off
Telephone No.: (0222) 220516
Postal Sales: Yes
Nearest Police Station: Cowbridge Road East
Cardiff (1 mile)
Police Force: South Wales
Police Telephone No.: (0222) 222111

GROUND INFORMATION
Away Supporters' Entrances: Grangetown End,
Sloper Road
Away Supporters' Sections: Grangetown End (Open)
Family Facilities: **Location of Stand**:
Below Grandstand and Canton Stand
Capacity of Stand: 3,271

ADMISSION INFO (1992/93 PRICES)
Adult Standing: Between £4.00 and £6.00
Adult Seating: Between £6.00 and £9.00
Child Standing: £2.00 - £4.00
Child Seating: £4.00 - £5.00
Programme Price: £1.00
FAX Number: (0222) 341148
Note: Adult prices vary depending on League position

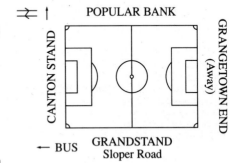

POPULAR BANK

CANTON STAND

GRANGETOWN END (Away)

← BUS   GRANDSTAND
Sloper Road

Travelling Supporters Information:
Routes: From North: Take A470 until Junction with Cardiff Bypass. Then 3rd exit at Roundabout A48 to
Port Talbot, after 2 miles take 1st exit at Roundabout A4161 (Cowbridge Road). Turn right (0.5 mile),
Lansdowne Road to Crossroads, turn right into Leckwith Road, then turn left (0.25 mile) into Sloper Road.
From East: Exit M4 taking A48 to Cardiff Bypass (then as North). From West: Take A4161 Cowbridge
Road (then as North).
Bus Services: Service No.2 - City Centre to Ground and Service No.1

CARLISLE UNITED FC

Founded: 1903
Turned Professional: 1903
Limited Company: 1921
Admitted to League: 1928
Former Name(s): Formed by Amalgamation
of Shaddongate Utd FC & Carlisle Red Rose FC
Nickname: 'Cumbrians'   'Blues'
Ground: Brunton Park, Warwick Road,
Carlisle   CA1 1LL

Record Attendance: 27,500 (5/1/57)
Colours: Shirts - Royal Blue
　　　　　　Shorts - White
Telephone No.: (0228) 26237
Ticket Information: (0228) 26237
Pitch Size: 117 × 78yds
Ground Capacity: 18,506
Seating Capacity: 2,162

GENERAL INFORMATION

Supporters Club Administrator: Colin
Barton
Address: 6 Old Post Office Court,
Devonshire Street, Carlisle
Telephone Number: (0228) 21261
Car Parking: Rear of Ground via St. Aidans
Road
Coach Parking: St. Aidans Road Car Park
Nearest Railway Station: Carlisle Citadel
(1 mile)
Nearest Bus Station: Lowther Street, Carlisle
Club Shop:
Opening Times: Weekdays 9.00-5.00
Saturdays 10.00-12.00
Telephone No.: (0228) 24014
Postal Sales: Yes
Nearest Police Station: Rickergate, Carlisle
(1.5 miles)
Police Force: Cumbria Constabulary
Police Telephone No.: (0228) 28191

GROUND INFORMATION

Away Supporters' Entrances: Turnstiles 22 to 25
Away Supporters' Sections: Visitors enclosure
Family Facilities: Location of Stand:
Main Stand
Capacity of Stand: 2,162

ADMISSION INFO (1992/93 PRICES)

Adult Standing: £5.00
Adult Seating: £7.00 or £7.50
Child Standing: £3.00
Child Seating: £4.00
Programme Price: £1.00
FAX Number: (0228) 30138

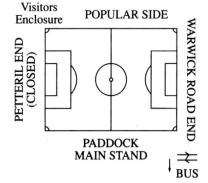

Travelling Supporters Information:
Routes: From North, South & East: Exit M6 Junction 43 and follow signs for Carlisle (A69) into Warwick
Road. From West: Take A69 straight into Warwick Road.

CHARLTON ATHLETIC FC

Founded: 1905	**Record Attendance**: 75,031 (12/2/38)
Turned Professional: 1920	**Colours**: Shirts - Red
Limited Company: 1984	Shorts - White
Admitted to League: 1921	**Telephone No.**: (081) 293-4567
Former Name(s): None	**Ticket Information**: (081) 293-4567
Nickname: 'Addicks'	**Pitch Size**: 112 × 73yds
Ground: The Valley, Floyd Road, Charlton	**Ground Capacity**: 12,000
London SE7 8BL	**Seating Capacity**: 9,000

GENERAL INFORMATION
Supporters Club Administrator:
Steve Clarke
Address: P.O. Box 387, London SE9 6EH
Telephone Number: (081) 304-1593
Car Parking: Street Parking
Coach Parking: By Police Direction
Nearest Railway Station: Charlton (2 mins walk)
Nearest Bus Station:
Club Shop:
Opening Times: Weekdays 10.00-6.00pm
Saturday 9.00-12.00
Telephone No.: (081) 293-4567
Postal Sales: Yes
Nearest Police Station: Greenwich (2 miles)
Police Force: Metropolitan
Police Telephone No.: (081) 853-8212

GROUND INFORMATION
Away Supporters' Entrances: Valley Grove
Away Supporters' Sections: South Stand
Family Facilities: **Location of Stand**:
West Stand
Capacity of Stand: 1,000

ADMISSION INFO (1992/93 PRICES)
Adult Standing: £8.00 - £9.00
Adult Seating: £10 Members   £12 Non-Members
Child Standing: £4.00 Members   £5 Non-Members
Child Seating: £5.00 Members   £6 Non-Members
Programme Price: £1.20
FAX Number: (081) 293-5143
(Charlton Athletic expect to start the 1992/93 Season playing at Upton Park until 31/10/92 - when they will move back to The Valley).

EAST TERRACE   BUS

HARVEY GARDENS
NORTH STAND

VALLEY GROVE
SOUTH STAND
(Away)

WEST STAND

Travelling Supporters Information:
Routes: From North: Follow city signs from A1/M1, then signs for Shoreditch & Whitechapel to A13. Follow Tilbury signs and use Blackwall Tunnel to A102M. Branch left after 1 mile and turn left at T-junction into A206. Turn right 0.5 mile into Charlton Church Lane, then left into Floyd Road; From East: Take A2 to Eltham for Blackwall Tunnel (then as North); From West: Take M4, then A4 to Central London then signs to Westminster & Embankment - Take A2 Dover Road then A206 (Woolwich). Turn right into Charlton Church Lane, then left into Floyd Road.
Bus Services: Services 53, 54, 75, 177 & 180 from City.

CHELSEA FC

Founded: 1905	**Record Attendance**: 82,905 (12/10/35)
Turned Professional: 1905	**Colours**: Shirts - Blue
Limited Company: 1905	Shorts - Blue
Admitted to League: 1905	**Telephone No.**: (071) 385-5545
Former Name(s): None	**Ticket Information**: (071) 385-5545
Nickname: 'Blues'	**Pitch Size**: 114 × 71yds
Ground: Stamford Bridge, Fulham Road,	**Ground Capacity**: 36,000
London SW6 1HS	**Seating Capacity**: 19,800

GENERAL INFORMATION

Supporters Club Administrator:
Pippa Robinson
Address: Contact via Club
Telephone Number: (071) 385-5545
Car Parking: Street Parking
Coach Parking: By Police Direction
Nearest Railway Station: Fulham Broadway
Nearest Tube Station: Fulham Broadway
(District)
Club Shop:
Opening Times: Weekdays 10.30-4.30
& Matchdays
Telephone No.: (071) 381-6172
Postal Sales: Yes
Nearest Police Station: Fulham
Police Force: Metropolitan
Police Telephone No.: (071) 385-1212

GROUND INFORMATION

Away Supporters' Entrances: Brittania Gate
Away Supporters' Sections: North Terrace (Open)
Family Facilities: Location of Stand:
East Stand (North Side)
Capacity of Stand: 2,010

ADMISSION INFO (1992/93 PRICES)

Adult Standing: £6-£7 member £7-£10 non-member
Adult Seating: £7.00 - £30.00: Depending on class
of game, place where seated, and whether or not you
are members. Also special rates in a Family Section.
Phone club for further details.
Child Standing: £4.00 - £5.00 Members
Child Seating: £5.00 - £6.00
Programme Price: £1.50
FAX Number: (071) 381-4831

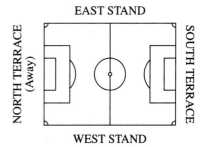

Travelling Supporters Information:

Routes: From North & East: Follow Central London signs from A1/M1 to Hyde Park Corner, then signs
Guildford (A3) to Knightsbridge (A4) after 1 mile turn left into Fulham Road; From South: Take A13 or
A24 then A219 to cross Putney Bridge and follow signs 'West End' (A304) to join A308 into Fulham
Road; From West: Take M4 then A4 to Central London, then signs to Westminster (A3220). After 0.75 mile
turn right at crossroads into Fulham Road.

CHESTER CITY FC

Founded: 1884
Turned Professional: 1902
Limited Company: 1909
Admitted to League: 1931
Former Name(s): Chester FC
Nickname: 'Blues' 'City'
Ground: The Deva Stadium, Bumpers Lane, Chester

Record Attendance: 20,500 (Sealand Road)
Colours: Shirts - Blue
Shorts - White
Telephone No.: (0244) 371376
Ticket Information: (0244) 373829
Pitch Size: 115 × 75yds
Ground Capacity: 6,000
Seating Capacity: 3,500 (Approximately)

GENERAL INFORMATION
Supporters Club Administrator: B. Hipkiss
Address: c/o Club
Telephone Number: (0244) 371376
Car Parking: Ample near ground
Coach Parking: Near Ground
Nearest Railway Station: Chester (1.5 miles)
Nearest Bus Station: Chester (0.75 mile)
Club Shop:
Opening Times: 9.00-4.30pm weekdays and Matchdays
Telephone No.: (0244) 317376
Postal Sales: Yes
Nearest Police Station: Chester (0.75 mile)
Police Force: Cheshire
Police Telephone No.: (0244) 350222

Note: The photograph is of the Old Stadium at Sealand Road as the new stadium was not completed at the time of publication.

GROUND INFORMATION
Away Supporters' Entrances: South Terrace
Away Supporters' Sections: South Terrace (Covered)
Family Facilities: **Location of Stand:**
Jewson Family Area
Capacity of Stand: 100 seats

ADMISSION INFO (1992/93 PRICES)
Adult Standing: £5.00
Adult Seating: £7.00   (concessions in
Child Standing: £4.00   Family Enclosure)
Child Seating: £5.50
Programme Price: £1.00
FAX Number: (0244) 661297

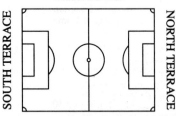

WEST STAND

SOUTH TERRACE

NORTH TERRACE

JEWSON FAMILY AREA
EAST STAND

Travelling Supporters Information:
Routes: From North: Take M56/A41 or A56 into Town Centre then follow Queensferry (A548) signs into Sealand Road. Turn left at Traffic Lights by Old Stadium into Bumpers Lane - ground is 0.5 mile at end of road; From East: Take A54 or A51 into Town Centre (then as North); From South: Take A41 or A483 into Town Centre (then as North); From West: Take A55/A494 or A548 and follow Queensferry signs towards Birkenhead A494 and after 1.25 miles bear left onto A548 (then as North).

CHESTERFIELD FC

Founded: 1866
Turned Professional: 1891
Limited Company: 1921
Admitted to League: 1899
Former Name(s): Chesterfield Town FC
Nickname: 'Spireites' 'Blues'
Ground: Recreation Ground, Saltergate, Chesterfield   S40 4SX

Record Attendance: 30,968 (7/4/39)
Colours: Shirts - Blue with White Pinstripes
Shorts - White
Telephone No.: (0246) 209765
Ticket Information: (0246) 209765
Pitch Size: 112 × 73yds
Ground Capacity: 11,308
Seating Capacity: 2,608

GENERAL INFORMATION
Supporters Club Administrator: Roy Frisby
Address: 76 Park Road, Chesterfield
Telephone Number: (0246) 39814
Car Parking: Saltergate Car Parks (0.5 mile)
Coach Parking: By Police Direction
Nearest Railway Station: Chesterfield (1ml)
Nearest Bus Station: Chesterfield
Club Shop:
Opening Times: Matchdays only
Telephone No.: (0246) 209765
Postal Sales: Yes
Nearest Police Station: Chesterfield (0.75ml)
Police Force: Derbyshire
Police Telephone No.: (0246) 220100

GROUND INFORMATION
Away Supporters' Entrances: Cross Street Turnstiles
Away Supporters' Sections: Cross Street End (Open)
Family Facilities: **Location of Stand**:
Main Stand - Saltergate Corner
Capacity of Stand: 400
Away Families: None

ADMISSION INFO (1992/93 PRICES)
Adult Standing: £5.00
Adult Seating: £6.00 - £7.00
Child Standing: £2.50
Child Seating: £3.00 - £3.50
Programme Price: £1.00
FAX Number: (0246) 556799

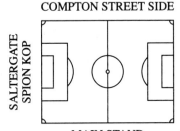

COMPTON STREET SIDE

SALTERGATE SPION KOP

CROSS STREET END (Away)

MAIN STAND
ST. MARGARET'S DRIVE

Travelling Supporters Information:
Routes: From North: Exit M1 Junction 30 then take A619 into Town Centre. Follow signs Old Brampton into Saltergate; From South & East: Take A617 into Town Centre (then as North); From West: Take A619 1st exit at Roundabout, (when into Town) into Foljambe Road and follow to end, turn right into Saltergate.

COLCHESTER UNITED FC

Founded: 1937
Former Name(s): The Eagles
Nickname: 'U's'
Ground: Layer Road Ground, Colchester CO2 7JJ
Record Attendance: 19,072 (27/11/48)

Colours: Shirts - Royal Blue/White
Shorts - Royal Blue
Telephone No.: (0206) 574042
Ticket Information: (0206) 574042
Pitch Size: 110 × 70yds
Ground Capacity: 7,223
Seating Capacity: 1,169

GENERAL INFORMATION
Supporters Club Administrator: Pete Tucker
Address: c/o Club
Telephone Number: (0206) 574042
Car Parking: Street Parking
Coach Parking: Boadicea Way (0.25 mile)
Nearest Railway Station: Colchester North (2 miles)
Nearest Bus Station: Colchester Town Centre
Club Shop:
Opening Times: Weekdays 9.00-5.00pm and most evenings
Telephone No.: (0206) 578978
Postal Sales: Yes
Nearest Police Station: Southway, Colchester (0.5 mile)
Police Force: Essex
Police Telephone No.: (0206) 762212

GROUND INFORMATION
Away Supporters' Entrances: Layer Road End Turnstiles
Away Supporters' Sections: Layer Rd. End (covered)

DISABLED SUPPORTERS INFORMATION
Wheelchairs: Accommodated by Prior Arrangement - in front of Main Stand
Disabled Toilets: None
The Blind: Commentaries Available

ADMISSION INFO (1992/93 PRICES)
Adult Standing: £5.00
Adult Seating: £6.00 - £7.50
Child Standing: £3.00
Child Seating: £4.00 - £5.50
Programme Price: £1.00
FAX Number: (0206) 48700

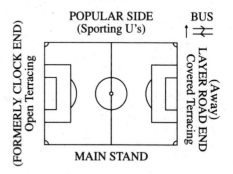

Travelling Supporters Information:
Routes: From North: Take A134/B1508 or A12 into Town Centre then follow signs to Layer (B1026) into Layer Road; From South: Take A12 and follow signs to Layer (B1026) into Layer Road; From West: Take A604 or A120 into Town Centre then follow Layer (B1026) signs into Layer Road.

COVENTRY CITY FC

Founded: 1883	**Record Attendance**: 51,455 (29/4/67)
Turned Professional: 1893	**Colours**: Shirts - Sky Blue/Navy & White
Limited Company: 1907	Shorts - Navy with Sky Blue & White
Admitted to League: 1919	Quarters
Former Name(s): Singers FC (1883-1898)	**Telephone No.**: (0203) 223535
Nickname: 'Sky Blues'	**Ticket Information**: (0203) 225545
Ground: Highfield Road Stadium,	**Pitch Size**: 110 × 76yds
King Richard Street, Coventry CV2 4FW	**Ground Capacity**: 25,311
	Seating Capacity: 17,650

GENERAL INFORMATION
Supporters Club Administrator: The Secretary
Address: Coventry City Supporters Club, Freehold Street, Coventry
Telephone Number: -
Car Parking: Street Parking
Coach Parking: Gosford Green Car Park
Nearest Railway Station: Coventry (1 mile)
Nearest Bus Station: Coventry (1 mile)
Club Shop: Thackhall Street
Opening Times: Daily except Sunday (Office hours)
Telephone No.: (0203) 257707
Postal Sales: Yes
Nearest Police Station: Little Park Street, Coventry (1 mile)
Police Force: West Midlands
Police Telephone No.: (0203) 539010

GROUND INFORMATION
Away Supporters' Entrances: Thackhall Street (Tickets from Away club)
Away Supporters' Sections: Sky Blue Stand & East Terrace
Family Facilities: Location of Stand: No special area
Capacity of Stand: -

ADMISSION INFO (1992/93 PRICES)
Adult Standing: £6.50 - £8.50
Adult Seating: £7.00 - £14.50   (Note : Prices vary
Child Standing: £4.00 - £5.50   depending on
Child Seating: £4.50 - £6.50   opponents)
Programme Price: £1.00
FAX Number: (0203) 630318
Note: Children/OAPs pay adult prices unless members

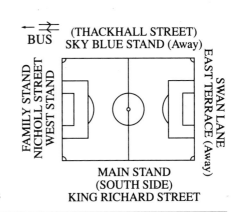

(THACKHALL STREET)
BUS   SKY BLUE STAND (Away)

FAMILY STAND
NICHOLL STREET
WEST STAND

EAST TERRACE (Away)
SWAN LANE

MAIN STAND
(SOUTH SIDE)
KING RICHARD STREET

Travelling Supporters Information:
Routes: From North, West & South: Exit M6 Junction 2. Take A4600 and follow signs for 'City Centre'. Follow this road for approximately 3 miles and, just under railway bridge turn right at traffic lights into Swan Lane. Stadium on left; From East: Take M45 then A45 to Ryton-on-Dunsmore. Take 3rd exit at roundabout (1.5 miles) A423, after 1.25 miles turn right (B4110), follow to T-junction, left then right into Swan Lane.
Bus Services: Service 25 from Railway Station to Bus Station. Services 16, 17, 32 & 33 from Bus Station.

CREWE ALEXANDRA FC

Founded: 1877
Turned Professional: 1893
Limited Company: 1892
Admitted to League: 1892
Former Name(s): None
Nickname: 'Railwaymen'
Ground: Gresty Road Ground, Crewe, Cheshire CW2 6EB

Record Attendance: 20,000 (30/1/60)
Colours: Shirts - Red
Shorts - White
Telephone No.: (0270) 213014
Ticket Information: (0270) 213014
Pitch Size: 112 × 74yds
Ground Capacity: 7,200
Seating Capacity: 1,200

GENERAL INFORMATION
Supporters Club Administrator: Glynn Steele
Address: 18 Gresty Road, Crewe
Telephone Number: (0270) 255206
Car Parking: Car Park at Ground (200 cars)
Coach Parking: Car Park at Ground
Nearest Railway Station: Crewe (5 mins.)
Nearest Bus Station: Crewe Town
Club Shop:
Opening Times: Monday-Friday 9.00-5.00 & Matchdays
Telephone No.: (0270) 213014
Postal Sales: Yes
Nearest Police Station: Crewe Town (1 mile)
Police Force: Cheshire
Police Telephone No.: (0270) 500222

GROUND INFORMATION
Away Supporters' Entrances: Gresty Road Entrances
Away Supporters' Sections: Gresty Road End
Family Facilities: Location of Stand:
Family Stand
Capacity of Stand: 200
Away Families: Yes

ADMISSION INFO (1992/93 PRICES)
Adult Standing: £5.00 - £5.50
Adult Seating: £7.00
Child Standing: £3.50 - £4.00
Child Seating: £5.00 (£2.50 in Family Stand - Members Only)
Programme Price: £1.00
FAX Number: (0270) 216320
Note : Family Area to be built for 1992/93 Season - full details not available at time of publication.

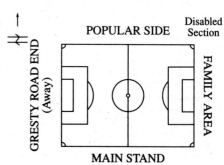

Travelling Supporters Information:
Routes: From North: Exit M6 Junction 17 take Crewe (A534) Road, and at Crewe roundabout follow Chester signs into Nantwich Road. Take left into Gresty Road; From South and East: Take A52 to A5020 to Crewe roundabout (then as North); From West: Take A534 into Crewe and turn right just before railway station into Gresty Road.

CRYSTAL PALACE FC

Founded: 1905	**Record Attendance**: 51,482 (11/5/79)
Turned Professional: 1905	**Colours**: Shirts - Red with Blue Stripes
Limited Company: 1905	Shorts - Red
Admitted to League: 1920	**Telephone No.**: (081) 653-4462
Former Name(s): None	**Ticket Information**: (081) 771-8841
Nickname: 'Eagles'	**Pitch Size**: 110 × 75yds
Ground: Selhurst Park, London, SE25 6PU	**Ground Capacity**: 30,312
	Seating Capacity: 15,712

GENERAL INFORMATION
Supporters Club Administrator:
Terry Byfield
Address: c/o Club
Telephone Number: (081) 653-4462
Car Parking: Street Parking/Sainsbury Car
Park near Ground
Coach Parking: Thornton Heath
Nearest Railway Station: Selhurst/Norwood
Junction/Thornton Heath
Nearest Bus Station: Norwood Junction
Club Shop:
Opening Times: Weekdays & Matchdays
9.30-5.30
Telephone No.: (081) 653-5584
Postal Sales: Yes
Nearest Police Station: South Norwood
(15 minutes walk)
Police Force: Metropolitan
Police Telephone No.: (081) 653-8568

GROUND INFORMATION
Away Supporters' Entrances: Park Road/Holmes-
dale Road
Away Supporters' Sections: Corner - Park Road &
Holmesdale Road (Open Terrace & Covered Seating)
Family Facilities: Location of Stand:
Members Stand (Clifton Road End)
Capacity of Stand: 4,600

ADMISSION INFO (1992/93 PRICES)
Adult Standing: £9.00
Adult Seating: £12.00 - £18.00
Child Standing: £5.00
Child Seating: £7.00 - £10.00
Programme Price: £1.30
FAX Number: (081) 771-5311
Note : Prices vary depending on the opponents

Travelling Supporters Information:
Routes: From North: Take M1/A1 to North Circular (A406) to Chiswick. Take South Circular (A205) to
Wandsworth, take A3 to A214 and follow signs to Streatham to A23. Turn left onto B273 (1 mile), follow to
end and turn left into High Street and into Whitehorse Lane; From East: Take A232 (Croydon Road) to
Shirley and join A215 (Northwood Road), after 2.25 miles take left into Whitehorse Lane; From South Take
A23 and follow signs Crystal Palace B266 through Thornton Heath into Whitehorse Lane; From West: Take
M4 to Chiswick (then as North).

DARLINGTON FC

Founded: 1883	**Record Attendance**: 21,023 (14/11/60)
Turned Professional: 1908	**Colours**: Shirts - White/Black
Limited Company: 1891	Shorts - Black
Admitted to League: 1921	**Telephone No.**: (0325) 465097
Former Name(s): None	**Ticket Information**: (0325) 467712
Nickname: 'Quakers'	**Pitch Size**: 110 × 74yds
Ground: Feethams Ground, Darlington	**Ground Capacity**: 9,957
DL1 5JB	**Seating Capacity**: 1,120

GENERAL INFORMATION
Supporters Club Administrator:
K.Lett
Address: 60 Harrison Terrace, Darlington
Telephone Number: (0325) 350161
Car Parking: Street Parking
Coach Parking: By Police direction
Nearest Railway Station: Darlington
Nearest Bus Station: Darlington Central
Club Shop:
Opening Times: Monday-Saturday 9.00-5.00
Telephone No.: (0325) 481212
Postal Sales: Yes
Nearest Police Station: Park Police Station,
Darlington (0.25 mile)
Police Force: Durham
Police Telephone No.: (0325) 467681

GROUND INFORMATION
Away Supporters' Entrances: Polam Lane Turnstiles
Away Supporters' Sections: West Terrace - Open
Family Facilities: **Location of Stand**:
West Stand
Capacity of Stand: 560
Away Families: Yes

ADMISSION INFO (1992/93 PRICES)
Adult Standing: £5.50
Adult Seating: £7.50   (£6.50 in Family Stand)
Child Standing: £2.50
Child Seating: £4.50   (£3.00 in Family Stand)
Programme Price: £1.00
FAX Number: (0325) 381377

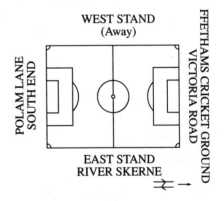

Travelling Supporters Information:
Routes: From North: Take A1(M) to A167 and follow road to Town Centre, then follow Northallerton signs to Victoria Road; From East: Take A67 to Town Centre (then as North); From South: Take A1(M) A66(M) into Town Centre and 3rd exit at roundabout into Victoria Road; From West: Take A67 into Town Centre and 3rd exit at roundabout into Victoria Road.

DERBY COUNTY FC

Founded: 1884	**Record Attendance**: 41,826 (20/9/69)
Turned Professional: 1884	**Colours**: Shirts - White
Limited Company: 1896	Shorts - Black
Admitted to League: 1888 (Founder)	**Telephone No.**: (0332) 40105
Former Name(s): None	**Ticket Information**: (0332) 40105
Nickname: 'Rams'	**Pitch Size**: 110 × 71yds
Ground: Baseball Ground, Shaftesbury	**Ground Capacity**: 23,800
Crescent, Derby DE3 8NB	**Seating Capacity**: 14,500

GENERAL INFORMATION
Supporters Club Administrator:
Mr. E. Hallam
Address: c/o Club
Telephone Number: (0332) 40105
Car Parking: Numerous Car Parks within
0.5 mile
Coach Parking: Russel St. Derby
Nearest Railway Station: Derby Midland
(1 mile) and Ramsline Halt (specials only)
Nearest Bus Station: Derby Central
Club Shop:
Opening Times: Weekdays 9.30-5.00
& Matches
Telephone No.: (0332) 292081
Postal Sales: Yes
Nearest Police Station: Cotton Lane, Derby
Police Force: Derbyshire
Police Telephone No.: (0332) 290100

GROUND INFORMATION
Away Supporters' Entrances: Osmaston Seating -
Turnstiles 51-55
Away Supporters' Sections: Osmaston Middle &
Lower Tier (seats)
Family Facilities: **Location of Stand**:
Vulcan Street End
Capacity of Stand: 3,500

ADMISSION INFO (1992/93 PRICES)
Adult Standing: £6.00
Adult Seating: £7.00 - £11.00
Child Standing: £3.00
Child Seating: £6.00
Programme Price: £1.00
FAX Number: (0332) 293514

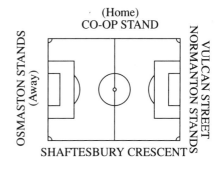

(Home)
CO-OP STAND

OSMASTON STANDS (Away)

VULCAN STREET NORMANTON STANDS

SHAFTESBURY CRESCENT

Travelling Supporters Information:
Routes: From North: Take A38 into City Centre then follow signs Melbourne (A514), turn right before
Railway Bridge into Shaftesbury Street; From South, East & West: Take Derby Ring Road to Junction
with A514 and follow signs to City Centre into Osmaston Road, after 1.25 miles take left turn into Shaftes-
bury Street.
Bus Services: Services 159, 188 and 189 pass near the Ground. Some Special services.

DONCASTER ROVERS FC

Founded: 1879
Turned Professional: 1885
Limited Company: 1920
Admitted to League: 1901
Former Name(s): None
Nickname: 'Rovers'
Ground: Belle Vue, Bawtry Road, Doncaster   DN4 5HT

Record Attendance: 37,149 (2/10/48)
Colours: Shirts - White with Red trim
Shorts - White
Telephone No.: (0302) 539441
Ticket Information: (0302) 539441
Pitch Size: 110 × 76yds
Ground Capacity: 6,535
Seating Capacity: 1,259

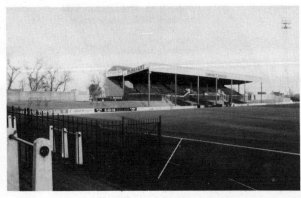

GENERAL INFORMATION
Supporters Club Administrator: K. Avis
Address: 64 Harrowden Road, Wheatley, Doncaster
Telephone Number: (0302) 365440
Car Parking: Large Car Park at Ground
Coach Parking: Car Park at Ground
Nearest Railway Station: Doncaster (1.5m)
Nearest Bus Station: Doncaster
Club Shop:
Opening Times: Tuesdays, Fridays & Matchdays 10.00-4.00
Telephone No.: (0302) 539441
Postal Sales: Yes
Nearest Police Station: College Road, Doncaster
Police Force: South Yorkshire
Police Telephone No.: (0302) 366744

GROUND INFORMATION
Away Supporters' Entrances: Turnstiles A & 1, 2, 3, 4, 'A' Block
Away Supporters' Sections: Rossington Road (Open) & Main Stand, 'A' Block
Family Facilities: **Location of Stand:** Main Stand
Capacity of Stand: -

ADMISSION INFO (1992/93 PRICES)
Adult Standing: £5.50
Adult Seating: £7.00
Child Standing: £3.30
Child Seating: £7.00
Programme Price: £0.90
FAX Number: (0302) 539679

POPULAR SIDE STAND

ROSSINGTON END (Away)

Enclosure
MAIN STAND
BAWTRY ROAD

BUS

Travelling Supporters Information:
Routes: From North: Take A1 to A638 into Town Centre, follow signs to Bawtry (A638), after 1.25 miles take 3rd exit from roundabout into Bawtry Road; From East: Take M18 to A630, after 2.75 miles take 1st exit at roundabout into A18, after 2.5 miles take 1st exit at roundabout into Bawtry Road; From South: Take M1 then M18, to A6182. After 2 miles 3rd exit at roundabout S/P 'Scunthorpe A18'. Then after 1.25 miles take 3rd exit at roundabout into Bawtry Road; From West: Take A635 into Town Centre and follow signs 'Bawtry' (then as South).

EVERTON FC

Founded: 1878
Turned Professional: 1885
Limited Company: 1892
Admitted to League: 1888 (Founder)
Former Name(s): St.Domingo's FC (1878-79)
Nickname: 'Blues'   'Toffeemen'
Ground: Goodison Park, Goodison Road.
Liverpool   L4 4EL

Record Attendance: 78,299 (18/9/48)
Colours: Shirts - Blue
              Shorts - White
Telephone No.: (051) 521-2020
Ticket Information: (051) 521-2020
Pitch Size: 112 × 78yds
Ground Capacity: 38,500
Seating Capacity: 36,500

GENERAL INFORMATION
Supporters Club Administrator: The Secretary
Address: 38 City Road, Liverpool 4
Telephone Number: (051) 525-2207
Car Parking: Corner of Priory and Utting Av.
Coach Parking: Priory Road
Nearest Railway Station: Liverpool Lime Street
Nearest Bus Station: Skelhorne Street, Liverpool
Club Shop:
Opening Times: Weekdays & Matchdays 9.00-5.00 and Evening matches
Telephone No.: (051) 521-2020
Postal Sales: Yes - Mail Order & Credit Card
Nearest Police Station: Walton Lane, Liverpool
Police Force: Merseyside
Police Telephone No.: (051) 709-6010

GROUND INFORMATION
Away Supporters' Entrances: Park End, Goodison Avenue Turnstiles
Away Supporters' Sections: Park End Stand
Family Facilities: **Location of Stand**:
In front of Main Stand
Capacity of Stand: 2,080

ADMISSION INFO (1992/93 PRICES)
Adult Standing: N/A - No Home standing
Adult Seating: £9.50 - £13.00
Child Standing: N/A - No Home standing
Child Seating: £3.00 - £4.00 (Child Concessions for
Programme Price: £1.20   Junior Members only)
FAX Number: (051) 523-9666
Note : Prices vary depending on the opponents

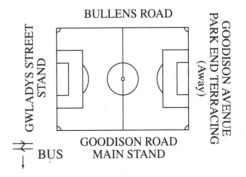

Travelling Supporters Information:
Routes: From North: Exit M6 junction 28. Take A58 Liverpool Road to A580 and follow into Walton Hall Avenue; From South & East: Exit M6 junction 21A to M62. At end of M62 turn right into Queen's Drive. After 3.75 miles turn left into Walton Hall Avenue; From North Wales: Cross Mersey into City Centre and follow signs to Preston (A580) into Walton Hall Avenue.
Bus Services: Service from City Centre - 30, 92, 92A/B, 93.

EXETER CITY FC

Founded: 1904
Turned Professional: 1908
Limited Company: 1908
Admitted to League: 1920
Former Name(s): Formed by amalgamation of St. Sidwell United FC & Exeter United FC
Nickname: 'Grecians'
Ground: St. James Park, Exeter   EX4 6PX

Record Attendance: 20,984 (4/3/31)
Colours: Shirts - Red & White Stripes
          Shorts - Black
Telephone No.: (0392) 54073
Ticket Information: (0392) 54073
Pitch Size: 114 × 73yds
Ground Capacity: 8,898
Seating Capacity: 1,608

GENERAL INFORMATION

Supporters Club Administrator: Mr M.A. Holladay
Address: c/o Club
Telephone Number: (0392) 59466
Car Parking: National Car Park Nearby
Coach Parking: Paris Street Bus Station
Nearest Railway Station: Exeter St. James Park (Adjacent)
Nearest Bus Station: Paris Street Bus Station
Club Shop:
Opening Times: Weekdays & Matchdays 9.00-5.00pm
Telephone No.: (0392) 54073
Postal Sales: Yes
Nearest Police Station: Heavitree Road, Exeter (0.5 mile)
Police Force: Devon & Cornwall
Police Telephone No.: (0392) 52101

GROUND INFORMATION

Away Supporters' Entrances: St. James Road Turnstiles
Away Supporters' Sections: St.James Road Enclosure
Family Facilities: Location of Stand:
Block C - Grandstand
Capacity of Stand: -

ADMISSION INFO (1992/93 PRICES)

Adult Standing: £5.00 - £6.00
Adult Seating: £8.00
Child Standing: £3.00
Child Seating: £5.00
Programme Price: £1.00
FAX Number: (0392) 425885

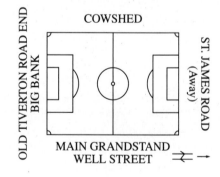

Travelling Supporters Information:
Routes: From North: Exit M5 junction 30 and follow signs to City Centre along Sidmouth Road and onto Heavitree Road, take 4th exit at roundabout into Western Way and 2nd exit Tiverton Road, next left into St. James Road; From East: Take A30 into Heavitree Road (then as North); From South & West: Take A38 and follow City Centre signs into Western Way and 3rd exit at roundabout into St. James Road.
Bus Services: Services A, D, J, K & S from City Centre,

FULHAM FC

Founded: 1879	**Record Attendance**: 49,335 (8/10/38)
Turned Professional: 1898	**Colours**: Shirts - White
Limited Company: 1903	Shorts - Black
Admitted to League: 1907	**Telephone No.**: (071) 736-6561
Former Name(s): Fulham St. Andrew's FC	**Ticket Information**: (071) 736-6561
(1879-1898)	**Pitch Size**: 110 × 75yds
Nickname: 'Cottagers'	**Ground Capacity**: 16,815
Ground: Craven Cottage, Stevenage Road,	**Seating Capacity**: 6,600
Fulham, London SW6 6HH	

GENERAL INFORMATION
Supporters Club Administrator: The Chairman
Address: c/o The Club
Telephone Number: (071) 736-6561
Car Parking: Street Parking
Coach Parking: Stevenage Road
Nearest Railway Station: Putney
Nearest Tube Station: Putney Bridge (District)
Club Shop:
Opening Times: Home Matchdays and by prior arrangement (phone)
Telephone No.: (071) 736-6561
Postal Sales: Yes
Nearest Police Station: Heckfield Place, Fulham
Police Force: Metropolitan
Police Telephone No.: (071) 741-6212

GROUND INFORMATION
Away Supporters' Entrances: Putney End
Away Supporters' Sections: Putney Terrace (Open)
Family Facilities: Location of Stand:
Miller Stand ('S' Block)
Capacity of Stand: 350
Away Families: Accommodated in Disabled Section

ADMISSION INFO (1992/93 PRICES)
Adult Standing: £6.00
Adult Seating: £9.00
Child Standing: £2.00
Child Seating: £3.00
Programme Price: £1.20
FAX Number: (071) 731-7047

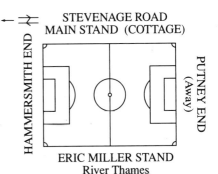

Travelling Supporters Information:
Routes: From North: Take A1/M1 to North Circular (A406) West to Neasden and follow signs Harlesdon A404, then Hammersmith A219. At Broadway follow Fulham sign and turn right (1 mile) into Harbord Street left at end to Ground; From South & East: Take South Circular (A205) and follow Putney Bridge sign (A219), Cross Bridge and follow Hammersmith signs for 0.5 mile, left into Bishops Park Road, then right at end; From West: Take M4 to A4 then branch left (2 miles) into Hammersmith Broadway (then as North).
Bus Services: Services 30, 74, 85, 95 & 220 from tube station to Ground.

GILLINGHAM FC

Founded: 1893	**Record Attendance**: 23,002 (10/1/48)
Turned Professional: 1894	**Colours**: Shirts - Blue
Limited Company: 1893	Shorts - White
Admitted to League: 1920	**Telephone No.**: (0634) 851854/851462
Former Name(s): New Brompton FC	**Ticket Information**: (0634) 8576828
1893-1913	**Pitch Size**: 114 × 75yds
Nickname: 'Gills'	**Ground Capacity**: 10,422
Ground: Priestfield Stadium, Redfern Avenue,	**Seating Capacity**: 1,225
Gillingham, Kent ME7 4DD	

GENERAL INFORMATION
Supporters Club Administrator:
The Chairman
Address: c/o Club
Telephone Number: (0634) 851854
Car Parking: Street Parking
Coach Parking: By Police Direction
Nearest Railway Station: Gillingham
Nearest Bus Station: Gillingham
Club Shop:
Opening Times: Weekdays & Matchdays
10.00-3.00
Telephone No.: (0634) 851462
Postal Sales: Yes
Nearest Police Station: Gillingham
Police Force: Kent
Police Telephone No.: (0634) 834488

GROUND INFORMATION
Away Supporters' Entrances: Redfern Avenue
Turnstiles
Away Supporters' Sections: Redfern Avenue Corner
(Gillingham End)
Family Facilities: **Location of Stand**:
Main Stand (Rainham End)
Capacity of Stand: 1,090

ADMISSION INFO (1992/93 PRICES)
Adult Standing: £6.00
Adult Seating: £8.00 - £10.00
Child Standing: £4.00
Child Seating: £6.00 - £10.00
Programme Price: £1.00
FAX Number: (0634) 850986

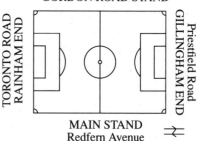

Travelling Supporters Information:
Routes: From All Parts: Exit M2 junction 4 and follow link road (dual carriageway) B278 to 3rd round-about. Turn left on to A2 (dual carriageway) across roundabout to traffic lights. Turn right Woodlands Road - after traffic lights. Ground 0.25 mile on left.

GRIMSBY TOWN FC

Founded: 1878	**Record Attendance**: 31,651 (20/2/37)
Turned Professional: 1890	**Colours**: Shirts - Black & White Stripes
Limited Company: 1890	Shorts - Black
Admitted to League: 1892	**Telephone No.**: (0472) 697111
Former Name(s): Grimsby Pelham FC (1879)	**Ticket Information**: (0472) 697111
Nickname: 'Mariners'	**Pitch Size**: 111 × 74yds
Ground: Blundell Park, Cleethorpes	**Ground Capacity**: 17,526
DN35 7PY	**Seating Capacity**: 5,021

GENERAL INFORMATION

Supporters Club Administrator:
Rachel Branson
Address: 26 Humberstone Road, Grimsby
Telephone Number: (0472) 360050
Car Parking: Street Parking
Coach Parking: Harrington Street -
Near Ground
Nearest Railway Station: Cleethorpes (1.5
miles), New Clee (0.5 mile - specials only)
Nearest Bus Station: Brighowgate, Grimsby
(4 miles)
Club Shop:
Opening Times: Monday-Friday 10.00-4.00
Match Saturdays 10.00-Kick-off
Telephone No.: (0472) 697111
Postal Sales: Yes
Nearest Police Station: Cleethorpes (Near
Railway Station) 1.5 miles
Police Force: Humberside
Police Telephone No.: (0472) 697131

GROUND INFORMATION

Away Supporters' Entrances: Harrington Street
Turnstiles 15-18 (Near Neville Street)
Away Supporters' Sections: Osmond Stand - Covered
standing and seats
Family Facilities: **Location of Stand**:
Main Stand (with access to family lounge)
Capacity of Stand: 120

ADMISSION INFO (1992/93 PRICES)

Adult Standing: £5.50
Adult Seating: £8.00
Child Standing: £3.50
Child Seating: £4.50
Programme Price: £1.00
FAX Number: (0472) 693665

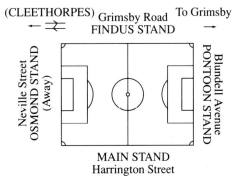

Travelling Supporters Information:

Routes: From All Parts except Lincolnshire and East Anglia: Take M180 to A180 follow signs to Grimsby/
Cleethorpes. A180 ends at roundabout (3rd in short distance after crossing Docks), take 2nd exit from roundabout over Railway flyover into Cleethorpes Road (A1098) and continue into Grimsby Road. After second
stretch of Dual Carriageway, Ground 0.5 mile on left; From Lincolnshire: Take A46 or A16 and follow
Cleethorpes signs along (A1098) Weelsby Road (2 miles) and take 1st exit at roundabout at end of Clee Road
into Grimsby Road. Ground 1.75 miles on right.

HALIFAX TOWN FC

Founded: 1911
Turned Professional: 1911
Limited Company: 1911
Admitted to League: 1921
Former Name(s): None
Nickname: 'Shaymen'
Ground: Shay Ground, Shay Syke, Halifax HX1 2YS

Record Attendance: 36,885 (14/2/53)
Colours: Shirts - Blue & White
Shorts - White
Telephone No.: (0422) 353423
Ticket Information: (0422) 353423
Pitch Size: 110 × 70yds
Ground Capacity: 8,049
Seating Capacity: 1,896

GENERAL INFORMATION
Supporters Club Administrator: None but contact A. Broughton - Commercial Manager
Address: Halifax Town Promotions, 7 Clare Road, Halifax
Telephone Number: (0422) 366593
Car Parking: Shaw Hill Car Park (Nearby)
Coach Parking: Calderdale Bus Depot (Shaw Hill)
Nearest Railway Station: Halifax (3 mins.)
Nearest Bus Station: Halifax
Club Shop:
Opening Times: Weekdays 9.30-5.00 (Except Thursdays) & Matchdays
Telephone No.: (0422) 366593
Postal Sales: Yes
Nearest Police Station: Halifax (0.25 mile)
Police Force: West Yorkshire
Police Telephone No.: (0422) 360333

GROUND INFORMATION
Away Supporters' Entrances: Shay Syke turnstiles
Away Supporters' Sections: Visitor's enclosure, Shay Syke
Family Facilities: **Location of Stand**: None Specified
Capacity of Stand: -
Away Families: No

ADMISSION INFO (1992/93 PRICES)
Adult Standing: £5.00
Adult Seating: £7.00
Child Standing: £3.00
Child Seating: £4.00
Programme Price: £1.00
FAX Number: (0422) 349487
Note : No Child concessions for Away Supporters

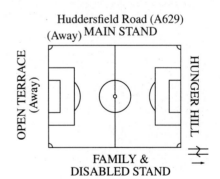

Huddersfield Road (A629)
(Away) MAIN STAND

OPEN TERRACE (Away)

HUNGER HILL

FAMILY & DISABLED STAND

Travelling Supporters Information:
Routes: From North: Take A629 to Halifax Town Centre. Take 2nd exit at roundabout into Broad Street and follow signs for Huddersfield (A629) into Skircoat Road; From South, East & West: Exit M62 junction 24 and follow Halifax (A629) signs to Town Centre into Skircoat Road for Ground.

HARTLEPOOL UNITED FC

Founded: 1908	**Record Attendance**: 17,426 (15/1/57)
Turned Professional: 1908	**Colours**: Shirts - Blue
Limited Company: 1908	Shorts - White
Admitted to League: 1921	**Telephone No.**: (0429) 272584
Former Name(s): Hartlepools United FC	**Ticket Information**: (0429) 222077
(1908-68); Hartlepool FC (1968-77)	**Pitch Size**: 113 × 77yds
Nickname: 'The Pool'	**Ground Capacity**: 9,607
Ground: Victoria Ground, Clarence Road,	**Seating Capacity**: 1,500
Hartlepool TS24 8BZ	

GENERAL INFORMATION
Supporters Club Administrator:
D. Lattimer
Address: 4 Friarage Gardens, Hartlepool
Telephone Number: -
Car Parking: Street Parking & rear of Clock Garage
Coach Parking: United Bus Station
Nearest Railway Station: Hartlepool Church Street (5 minutes walk)
Nearest Bus Station: United Bus Station
Club Shop:
Opening Times: Weekdays 9.00-5.00
Saturdays 9.00-2.30
Telephone No.: (0429) 222077
Postal Sales: Yes
Nearest Police Station: Avenue Road, Hartlepool
Police Force: Cleveland
Police Telephone No.: (0429) 221151

GROUND INFORMATION
Away Supporters' Entrances: Clarence Road Turnstiles 1, 2 & 3
Away Supporters' Sections: Town End, Clarence Rd.
Family Facilities: **Location of Stand**:
None
Capacity of Stand: -

ADMISSION INFO (1992/93 PRICES)
Adult Standing: £6.00
Adult Seating: £8.00
Child Standing: £4.00
Child Seating: £5.00
Programme Price: £1.00
FAX Number: (0429) 863007

Clarence Road (Away)   BUS
TOWN END

RINK END   TOWN END

OFFICIAL   MILL HOUSE STAND
CAR PARK   RABY ROAD

Travelling Supporters Information:
Routes: From North: Take A1/A19 then A179 towards Hartlepool to Hart. Straight across traffic lights (2.5 miles) to cross-roads, then turn left into Clarence Road; From South & West: Take A1/A19 or A689 into Town Centre then bear left into Clarence Road.

HEREFORD UNITED FC

Founded: 1924
Turned Professional: 1924
Limited Company: 1939
Admitted to League: 1972
Former Name(s): None
Nickname: 'United'
Ground: Edgar Street, Hereford   HR4 9JU

Record Attendance: 18,114 (4/1/58)
Colours: Shirts - White
             Shorts - Black
Telephone No.: (0432) 276666
Ticket Information: (0432) 276666
Pitch Size: 111 × 74yds
Ground Capacity: 13,777
Seating Capacity: 2,897

GENERAL INFORMATION

Supporters Club Administrator:
K. Benjimen
Address: c/o Club
Telephone Number: (0432) 265005
Car Parking: Merton Meadow & Edgar Street Car Parks
Coach Parking: Cattle Market (Near Ground)
Nearest Railway Station: Hereford (0.5 mile)
Nearest Bus Station: Commercial Road, Hereford
Club Shop:
Opening Times: Matchdays & Weekdays via Commercial Office
Telephone No.: (0432) 276666
Postal Sales: Yes
Nearest Police Station: Bath Street, Hereford
Police Force: Hereford
Police Telephone No.: (0432) 276422

GROUND INFORMATION

Away Supporters' Entrances: Blackfriars Street and Edgar Street
Away Supporters' Sections: Blackfriars Street End
Family Facilities: **Location of Stand**: Edgar Street Side
Capacity of Stand: 300

ADMISSION INFO (1992/93 PRICES)

Adult Standing: £5.00
Adult Seating: £7.00
Child Standing: £4.00
Child Seating: £5.00
Programme Price: £1.00
FAX Number: (0432) 341359

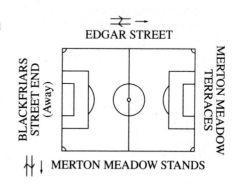

EDGAR STREET

BLACKFRIARS STREET END (Away)

MERTON MEADOW TERRACES

MERTON MEADOW STANDS

Travelling Supporters Information:
Routes: From North: Follow A49 Hereford signs straight into Edgar Street; From East: Take A465 or A438 into Hereford Town Centre, then follow signs for Leominster (A49) into Edgar Street; From South: Take A49 or A465 into Town Centre (then as East); From West: Take A438 into Town Centre (then as East).

HUDDERSFIELD TOWN FC

Founded: 1908
Turned Professional: 1908
Limited Company: 1908
Admitted to League: 1910
Former Name(s): None
Nickname: 'Terriers'
Ground: Leeds Road, Huddersfield
HD1 6PE

Record Attendance: 67,037 (27/2/32)
Colours: Shirts - Blue & White Stripes
Shorts - White
Telephone No.: (0484) 420335
Ticket Information: (0484) 420335
Pitch Size: 115 × 75yds
Ground Capacity: 17,010
Seating Capacity: 5,340

GENERAL INFORMATION
Supporters Club Administrator:
Mrs A. Sedgwick
Address: c/o Club
Telephone Number: (0484) 420335
Car Parking: Car Park for 1,000 cars adjacent
Coach Parking: Adjacent Car Park
Nearest Railway Station: Huddersfield
(1.25 miles)
Nearest Bus Station: Huddersfield
Club Shop:
Opening Times: Weekdays and Matchdays
9.00-6.00pm (8.00pm on Thursdays)
Telephone No.: (0484) 534867
Postal Sales: Yes
Nearest Police Station: Huddersfield (1 mile)
Police Force: West Yorkshire
Police Telephone No.: (0484) 422122

GROUND INFORMATION
Away Supporters' Entrances: Turnstiles 9-10 (seats);
Turnstiles 11-18 (standing)
Away Supporters' Sections: Dalton Bank Terrace
(Open)
Family Facilities: **Location of Stand**:
Leeds Road End
Capacity of Stand: 1,900

ADMISSION INFO (1991/92 PRICES)
Adult Standing: £5.00
Adult Seating: £8.00
Child Standing: £3.50
Child Seating: £4.50
Programme Price: £1.00
FAX Number: (0484) 515122

Traveling Supporters Information:
Routes: From North, East & West: Exit M62 junction 25 and take the A644 and A62 following Hudders-
field signs. Stadium on left side of A62 (Leeds Road) 1 mile before town centre; From South: Leave M1 at
Junction 38 then follow A637/A642 to Huddersfield. At Ring Road follow signs A62 (Leeds Road) Stadium
on right (1 mile).
Bus Services: Services 220, 221, 201/2/3

HULL CITY FC

<table>
<tr><td>

Founded: 1904
Turned Professional: 1904
Limited Company: 1904
Admitted to League: 1905
Former Name(s): None
Nickname: 'Tigers'
Ground: Boothferry Park, Boothferry Road,
Hull   HU4 6EU

</td><td>

Record Attendance: 55,019 (26/2/49)
Colours: Shirts - Amber & Black Stripes
            Amber Sleeves
            Shorts - Black
Telephone No.: (0482) 51119
Ticket Information: (0482) 51119
Pitch Size: 112 × 72yds
Ground Capacity: 17,380
Seating Capacity: 5,294

</td></tr>
</table>

GENERAL INFORMATION
Supporters Club Administrator:
S.C.A.Riby
Address: c/o Club
Telephone Number: (0482) 446878
Car Parking: Limited Parking at Ground
Street Parking
Coach Parking: At Ground
Nearest Railway Station: Hull Paragon
(1.5 miles)
Nearest Bus Station: Ferensway, Hull
(1.5 miles)
Club Shop: Paragon Square, Hull
Opening Times: Weekdays 9.30-4.30
Matchdays 10.00-3.00 - Ground
Telephone No.: (0482) 51119/28297
Postal Sales: Yes
Nearest Police Station: Priory Road, Hull
(2 miles)
Police Force: Humberside
Police Telephone No.: (0482) 512111

GROUND INFORMATION
Away Supporters' Entrances: North Stand Turnstiles
Away Supporters' Sections: Visitor's enclosure,
North Stand
Family Facilities: **Location of Stand**:
Main Stand
Capacity of Stand: 568

ADMISSION INFO (1992/93 PRICES)
Adult Standing: £6.00
Adult Seating: £7.00 - £8.00
Child Standing: £2.00
Child Seating: £3.00 - £4.00
Programme Price: £1.00
FAX Number: (0482) 565752

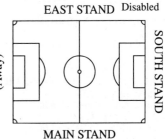

Travelling Supporters Information:
Routes: From North: Take A1 or A19 then A1079 into City Centre and follow signs for Leeds (A63) into
Anlaby Road. At roundabout (1 mile) take 1st exit into Boothferry Road; From West: Take M62 to A63 to
Hull. Fork left after Ferriby Crest Motel to Humber Bridge roundabout, then take 1st exit to Boothferry Road
(Ground 1.5 miles). Do NOT follow Clive Sullivan way; From South: Non-scenic alternative route take
M18 to M62 (then as West). Or use motorways M1 to M18 then M180 and follow signs over Humber Bridge
(Toll), take 2nd exit at roundabout (A63) towards Boothferry Road (Ground 1.5 miles).

IPSWICH TOWN FC

Founded: 1887
Turned Professional: 1936
Limited Company: 1936
Admitted to League: 1938
Former Name(s): None
Nickname: 'Town' 'Super Blues'
Ground: Portman Road, Ipswich   IP1 2DA

Record Attendance: 38,010 (8/3/75)
Colours: Shirts - Blue
    Shorts - White
Telephone No.: (0473) 219211
Ticket Information: (0473) 219211
Pitch Size: 112 × 70yds
Ground Capacity: 22,500 (approximately)
Seating Capacity: 22,500 (approximately)

GENERAL INFORMATION
Supporters Club Administrator:
Mr. G. Dodson
Address: c/o Club
Telephone Number: (0473) 219211
Car Parking: Portman Road and Portman Walk Car Parks
Coach Parking: Portman Walk
Nearest Railway Station: Ipswich (5 mins)
Nearest Bus Station: Ipswich
Club Shop:
Opening Times: Weekdays & Matchdays 9.00-5.00
Telephone No.: (0473) 219211
Postal Sales: Yes
Nearest Police Station: Civic Drive, Ipswich (5 minutes walk)
Police Force: Suffolk
Police Telephone No.: (0473) 55811

GROUND INFORMATION
Away Supporters' Entrances: Portman Walk Turnstiles
Away Supporters' Sections: Visitor's section, North Stand (Covered)
Family Facilities: Location of Stand:
South side of Pioneer Stand
Capacity of Stand: 2,200

ADMISSION INFO (1992/93 PRICES)
Adult Standing: N/A
Adult Seating: £7.00 - £18.00
Child Standing: N/A
Child Seating: £4.00 - £12.00
Programme Price: £1.00
FAX Number: (0473) 226835

PORTMAN ROAD
PORTMAN STAND

(Away)
PORTMAN WALK
NORTH STAND

CHURCHMAN'S END
SOUTH STAND

PIONEER STAND
CONSTANTINE ROAD

Travelling Supporters Information:
Routes: From North & West: Take A45 following signs for Ipswich West only. Proceed through Post House traffic lights and at 2nd roundabout turn right into West End Road, ground 0.25 mile along on left; From South: Follow signs for Ipswich West then as North and West.

LEEDS UNITED FC

Founded: 1919	**Record Attendance**: 57,892 (15/3/67)
Turned Professional: 1919	**Colours**: Shirts - White
Limited Company: 1919	Shorts - White
Admitted to League: 1920	**Telephone No.**: (0532) 716037
Former Name(s): Formed after Leeds City FC	**Ticket Information**: (0532) 710710
wound up for 'Irregular Practices'	**Pitch Size**: 117 × 76yds
Nickname: 'United'	**Ground Capacity**: 32,000
Ground: Elland Road, Leeds LS11 0ES	**Seating Capacity**: 16,500

GENERAL INFORMATION
Supporters Club Administrator:
Eric Carlile
Address: c/o Club
Telephone Number: (0532) 716037
Car Parking: Large Car Parks (Adjacent)
Coach Parking: By Police Direction
Nearest Railway Station: Leeds City
Nearest Bus Station: Leeds City Centre -
Specials from Swinegate
Club Shop:
Opening Times: Weekdays 9.15-5.00,
Matchdays 9.15-Kick-off
Telephone No.: (0532) 706844
Postal Sales: Yes (send SAE)
Nearest Police Station: Holbeck, Leeds
(3 miles)
Police Force: West Yorkshire
Police Telephone No.: (0532) 435353

GROUND INFORMATION
Away Supporters' Entrances: Lowfield Road
Away Supporters' Sections: Lowfield Road - Pen 5
(Open)
Family Facilities: **Location of Stand**:
South Stand Paddock
Capacity of Stand: 2,500

ADMISSION INFO (1992/93 PRICES)
Adult Standing: £7.50
Adult Seating: £13.00, £14.00 or £18.00
Child Standing: Half-price for Members only
Child Seating: Half-price for Members only
Programme Price: £1.00
FAX Number: (0532) 706560
Note : Adult standing limited to Season Ticket holders

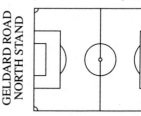

LOWFIELD ROAD STAND
(Away)

GELDARD ROAD NORTH STAND

ELLAND ROAD SOUTH STAND

WEST STAND

Travelling Supporters Information:
Routes: From North: Take A58 or A61 into City Centre and follow signs to M621; Leave Motorway after 1.5 miles and exit roundabout on to A643 into Elland Road; From North-East: Take A63 or A64 into City Centre (then as North); From South: Take M1 to M621 (then as North); From West: Take M62 to M621 (then as North).

LEICESTER CITY FC

Founded: 1884	**Record Attendance**: 47,298 (18/2/28)
Turned Professional: 1894	**Colours**: Shirts - Blue with White Collars
Limited Company: 1894	Shorts - White
Admitted to League: 1894	**Telephone No.**: (0533) 555000
Former Name(s): Leicester Fosse FC	**Ticket Information**: (0533) 555000
(1884-1919)	**Pitch Size**: 112 × 75yds
Nickname: 'Filberts' 'Foxes'	**Ground Capacity**: 22,181
Ground: City Stadium, Filbert Street,	**Seating Capacity**: 12,833
Leicester LE2 7FL	

GENERAL INFORMATION
Supporters Club Administrator:
C. Ginetta
Address: c/o Club
Telephone Number: (0533) 555000
Car Parking: NCP Car Park (5 mins. walk)
& Street Parking
Coach Parking: Western Boulevard
Nearest Railway Station: Leicester (1 mile)
Nearest Bus Station: St.Margaret's (1 mile)
Club Shop:
Opening Times: Weekdays 9.00-5.00
(closes for lunch), Matchdays 10.00-3.00
Telephone No.: (0533) 555000
Postal Sales: Yes
Nearest Police Station: Charles Street,
Leicester
Police Force: Leicester
Police Telephone No.: (0533) 530066

GROUND INFORMATION
Away Supporters' Entrances: East Stand, Block T
Turnstiles
Away Supporters' Sections: Spion Kop enclosure
(covered)/Block T East Stand
Family Facilities: Location of Stand:
By Member's Stand
Capacity of Stand: 3,600

ADMISSION INFO (1992/93 PRICES)
Adult Standing: £5.50
Adult Seating: £7.50 - £11.00
Child Standing: £2.50 Members Only
Child Seating: £4.00 - £6.00
Programme Price: £1.00
FAX Number: (0533) 470585

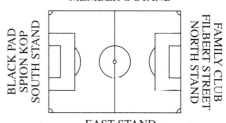

MEMBER'S STAND

BLACK PAD | SPION KOP SOUTH STAND

FAMILY CLUB | FILBERT STREET | NORTH STAND

BLOCK T. (Away)   EAST STAND BURNMOOR STREET

Travelling Supporters Information:
Routes: From North: Take A46/A607 into City Centre or exit M1 junction 22 for City Centre, follow
'Rugby' signs into Almond Road, turn right at end into Aylestone Road, turn left into Walnut Street and left
again into Filbert Street; From East: Take A47 into City Centre (then as for North); From South: Exit M1
junction 21 and take A46, turn right 0.75 mile after Railway bridge into Upperton Road, then right into Filbert
Street; From West: Take M69 to City Centre (then as North).

LEYTON ORIENT FC

Founded: 1881
Turned Professional: 1903
Limited Company: 1906
Admitted to League: 1905
Former Name(s): Glyn Cricket & Football Club (1881/6); Eagle FC (1886/8); Clapton Orient FC (1888/1946); Leyton Orient FC (1946/66); Orient FC (1966/87)
Nickname: 'O's'

Record Attendance: 34,345 (25/1/64)
Colours: Shirts - Red
Shorts - White
Telephone No.: (081) 539-2223
Ticket Information: (081) 539-2223
Pitch Size: 115 × 80yds
Ground Capacity: 18,869
Seating Capacity: 7,171

Ground: Leyton Stadium, Brisbane Road, Leyton, London   E10 5NE

GENERAL INFORMATION

Supporters Club Administrator: D.Dodd
Address: c/o Club
Telephone Number: (081) 539-6156
Car Parking: NCP Brisbane Road & Street Parking
Coach Parking: By Police Direction
Nearest Railway Station: Leyton Midland Road (0.5 mile)
Nearest Tube Station: Leyton (Central)
Club Shop:
Opening Times: Monday-Friday (Wednesday closed) 10.00-4.30pm
Telephone No.: (081) 539-2223
Postal Sales: Yes
Nearest Police Station: Francis Road, Leyton, London   E10
Police Force: Metropolitan
Police Telephone No.: (081) 556-8855

GROUND INFORMATION

Away Supporters' Entrances: South Terrace Turnstiles
Away Supporters' Sections: South Terrace (Open)
Family Facilities: **Location of Stand**: North Wing
Capacity of Stand: not specified

ADMISSION INFO (1992/93 PRICES)

Adult Standing: £5.50
Adult Seating: £6.50 - £9.50
Child Standing: £3.00
Child Seating: £3.50 - £5.50
Programme Price: £1.00
FAX Number: (081) 539-4390

```
                  OLIVER ROAD
                   WEST STAND
  BUCKINGHAM ROAD                      WINDSOR ROAD
  SOUTH TERRACE (Away)                 NORTH TERRACE

                   MAIN STAND
                  BRISBANE ROAD
```

Travelling Supporters Information:
Routes: From North & West: Take A406 North Circular and follow signs Chelmsford, to Edmonton, after 2.5 miles 3rd exit at roundabout towards Leyton (A112). Pass railway station and turn right (0.5 mile) into Windsor Road and left into Brisbane Road; From East: Follow A12 to London then City for Leytonstone follow Hackney signs into Grove Road, cross Main Road into Ruckholt Road and turn right into Leyton High Road, turn left (0.25 mile) into Buckingham Road, then left into Brisbane Road; From South: Take A102M through Blackwall Tunnel and follow signs to Newmarket (A102) to join A11 to Stratford, then signs Stratford Station into Leyton Road to railway station (then as North).

LINCOLN CITY FC

Founded: 1883	**Record Attendance**: 23,196 (15/11/67)
Turned Professional: 1892	**Colours**: Shirts - Red & White Stripes
Limited Company: 1892	Shorts - Black
Admitted to League: 1892	**Telephone No.**: (0522) 522224/510263
Former Name(s): None	**Ticket Information**: (0522) 522224/510263
Nickname: 'Red Imps'	**Pitch Size**: 110 × 75yds
Ground: Sincil Bank, Lincoln LN5 8LD	**Ground Capacity**: 11,500
	Seating Capacity: 2,050

GENERAL INFORMATION
Supporters Club Administrator: -
Address: c/o Club
Telephone Number: (0522) 522224/510263
Car Parking: Adjacent (£1.00)
Coach Parking: South Common (300 yards)
Nearest Railway Station: Lincoln Central
Nearest Tube Station: Lincoln Central
Club Shop: At Ground, St. Andrews Stand
Opening Times: Weekdays & Matchdays
9.00-5.00
Telephone No.: (0522) 522224/510263
Postal Sales: Yes
Nearest Police Station: West Parade, Lincoln
(1.5 miles)
Police Force: Lincolnshire
Police Telephone No.: (0522) 529911

GROUND INFORMATION
Away Supporters' Entrances: South-west Corner,
Sincil Bank
Away Supporters' Sections: South-west Corner,
Sincil Bank (open)
Family Facilities: Location of Stand:
Family Stand
Capacity of Stand: 1,450

ADMISSION INFO (1992/93 PRICES)
Adult Standing: £4.50 - £5.00
Adult Seating: £5.00 - £6.80
Child Standing: £3.00 (From 70p with an adult)
Child Seating: £4.50 - £5.00
Programme Price: £1.00
FAX Number: (0522) 520564

```
            SINCIL BANK
          (Away)      (Home)
   S                              S
   O                              T
   U                              A
   T                              C
   H                              E
                                  Y
   P                              
   A                              W
   R                              E
   K                              S
                                  T
   S                              
   T                              S
   A                              T
   N                              A
   D                              N
                                  D
         ST. ANDREW'S STAND
```

Travelling Supporters Information:
Routes: From East: Take A46 or A158 into City Centre following Newark (A46) signs into High Street. Pass under railway bridge and take next left (Scorer Street & Cross Street) for Ground; From North & West: Take A15 or A57 into City Centre then as East; From South: Take A1 to A46 for City Centre then into High Street and turn right into Scorer Street, then right again into Cross Street for Ground.

LIVERPOOL FC

Founded: 1892
Turned Professional: 1892
Limited Company: 1892
Admitted to League: 1893
Former Name(s): None
Nickname: 'Reds'
Ground: Anfield Road, Liverpool   L4 0TH

Record Attendance: 61,905 (2/2/52)
Colours: Shirts - Red with White Markings
Shorts - Red with White Markings
Telephone No.: (051) 263-2361
Ticket Information: (051) 260-8680
Pitch Size: 110 × 75yds
Ground Capacity: 44,431
Seating Capacity: 27,951

GENERAL INFORMATION
Supporters Club Administrator: -
Address: Liverpool Supporters Club, Lower Breck Road, Anfield, Liverpool
Telephone Number: (051) 263-6386
Car Parking: Stanley Park car park (adjacent)
Coach Parking: Priory Rd. & Pinehurst Ave.
Nearest Railway Station: Kirkdale
Nearest Bus Station: Skelhorne Street, Liverpool
Club Shop:
Opening Times: Monday-Saturday 9.30-5.30
Telephone No.: (051) 263-1760
Postal Sales: Yes
Nearest Police Station: Walton Lane, Liverpool (1.5 miles)
Police Force: Merseyside
Police Telephone No.: (051) 709-6010

GROUND INFORMATION
Away Supporters' Entrances: Anfield Road
Away Supporters' Sections: Visitors Section, Anfield Road (Covered)
Family Facilities: Location of Stand: Anfield Road End
Capacity of Stand: 1,300

ADMISSION INFO (1991/92 PRICES)
Adult Standing: Grade 'A' games £8   Grade 'B' £7
Adult Seating: Grade 'A' games £13   Grade 'B' £12
Child Standing: Grade 'A' £4.50   Grade 'B' £4.00
Child Seating: Grade 'A' games £5.50   Grade 'B' £5
Programme Price: £1.00
FAX Number: (051) 260-8813
Note : Prices vary depending on opponents

```
                KEMLYN ROAD STAND
    A                                          W S
    N                                          A P
    F                                          L I
    I                                          T O
    E                                          O N
    L                                          N
    D                                          B K
    R                                          R O
    O                                          E P
    A                                          C
    D                                          K
   (Away)                                      R
                                               O
                                               A
                                               D
            PADDOCK ENCLOSURE
              MAIN STAND          ⇄ ↓
             LOTHAIR ROAD
```

Travelling Supporters Information:
Routes: From North: Exit M6 junction 28 and follow Liverpool A58 signs into Walton Hall Avenue, pass Stanley Park and turn left into Anfield Road; From South & East: Take M62 to end of motorway then turn right into Queen's Drive (A5058) and turn left (3 miles) into Utting Avenue, after 1 mile turn right into Anfield Road; From North Wales: Take Mersey Tunnel into City Centre and follow signs to Preston (A580) into Walton Hall Avenue, turn right into Anfield Road before Stanley Park.

LUTON TOWN FC

Founded: 1885
Turned Professional: 1890
Limited Company: 1897
Admitted to League: 1897
Former Name(s): Formed by amalgamation of Wanderers FC & Excelsior FC
Nickname: 'Hatters'
Ground: Kenilworth Road Stadium, 1 Maple Road, Luton   LU4 8AW

Record Attendance: 30,069 (4/3/59)
Colours: Shirts - White/Royal Blue/Orange
  Shorts - Blue/Orange/White
Telephone No.: (0582) 411622
Ticket Information: (0582) 30748
Pitch Size: 110 × 72yds
Ground Capacity: 13,466
Seating Capacity: 9,116

GENERAL INFORMATION
Supporters Club Administrator: Mrs.P.Gray
Address: 19 Kingsdown Avenue, Luton, Beds
Telephone Number: (0582) 391574
Car Parking: Street Parking
Coach Parking: Luton Bus Station
Nearest Railway Station: Luton (1 mile)
Nearest Tube Station: Bute Street, Luton
Club Shop: Oak Road
Opening Times: 9.00-5.00
Telephone No.: (0582) 411622
Postal Sales: Yes
Nearest Police Station:Buxton Road, Luton (0.75 mile)
Police Force: Bedfordshire
Police Telephone No.: (0582) 401212

GROUND INFORMATION
Away Supporters' Entrances: Oak Road
Away Supporters' Sections: Oak Stand
Family Facilities: Location of Stand: Kenilworth Stand
Capacity of Stand: 5,802

ADMISSION INFO (1992/93 PRICES)
Adult Standing: £5.50 - £6.00
Adult Seating: £6.00 - £13.00
Child Standing: £3.00 £3.30
Child Seating: £3.50 - £6.50
Programme Price: £1.50
FAX Number: (0582) 405070
Note : Lower prices apply when tickets are purchased at least 14 days before the game.

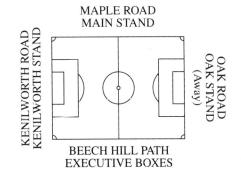

Travelling Supporters Information:
Routes: From North & West: Exit M1 junction 11 and follow signs to Luton (A505) into Dunstable Road. Follow one-way system and turn right back towards Dunstable, take first left into Oak Road; From South & East: Exit M1 junction 10 (or A6/A612) into Luton Town Centre and follow signs into Dunstable Road. After railway bridge take sixth turning on left into Oak Road.

MAIDSTONE UNITED FC

Founded: 1897	**Record Attendance**: Not Applicable
Turned Professional: 1971	**Colours**: Shirts - Gold
Limited Company: 1982	Shorts - Black
Admitted to League: 1989	**Telephone No.**: (0622) 754403
Former Name(s): None	**Ticket Information**: (0622) 754403
Nickname: 'The Stones'	**Pitch Size**: 110 × 75yds
Ground: Watling Street, Stone, Dartford,	**Ground Capacity**: 5,250
Kent	**Seating Capacity**: 720

GENERAL INFORMATION
Supporters Club Administrator: None
Address: -
Telephone Number: -
Car Parking: Street Parking Only
Coach Parking: Adjacent to Ground
Nearest Railway Station: Dartford (1.5 mls)
Nearest Bus Station: Dartford
Club Shop:
Opening Times: Matchdays Only
Telephone No.: (0622) 670474
Postal Sales: Yes
Nearest Police Station: Dartford (1.5 miles)
Police Force: Kent
Police Telephone No.: (0322) 227202

GROUND INFORMATION
Away Supporters' Entrances: St. John's Road
Turnstiles
Away Supporters' Sections: St. John's Road Side
Family Facilities: **Location of Stand**:
Family Terrace in front of Main Stand
Capacity of Stand: 720

ADMISSION INFO (1991/92 PRICES)
Adult Standing: £5.00
Adult Seating: £8.00 (Members only)
Child Standing: £3.00
Child Seating: £6.00 (Members only)
Programme Price: £1.00
FAX Number: (0622) 685803

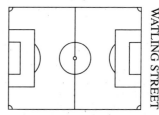

ST. JOHN'S ROAD
(Away)

WATLING STREET

MAIN STAND

Note: At the time of publication, the future of Maidstone United FC was in doubt due to Financial problems.

Travelling Supporters Information:
Routes: From Town Centre/Railway Station proceed up East Hill and take 3rd right into Watling Street via Dartford Tunnel A2 Dartford turn-off - floodlights visible from roundabout - Princes Hotel; From Kent Coast: A2/M2 turn-off for Greenhithe/Stone left at roundabout and right at traffic lights into Watling Street.

MANCHESTER CITY FC

Founded: 1887	**Record Attendance**: 84,569 (3/3/34)
Turned Professional: 1887	**Colours**: Shirts - Sky Blue
Limited Company: 1894	Shorts - White
Admitted to League: 1892	**Telephone No.**: (061) 226-1191
Former Name(s): Ardwick FC (1887-94)	**Ticket Information**: (061) 226-2224
Nickname: 'Citizens' 'City' 'Blues'	**Pitch Size**: 117 × 76yds
Ground: Maine Road, Moss Side,	**Ground Capacity**: 34,400
Manchester M14 7WN	**Seating Capacity**: 16,545

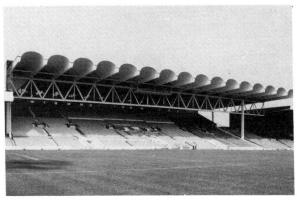

GENERAL INFORMATION

Supporters Club Administrator: Frank Horrocks
Address: Manchester City Supporter's Club, Maine Road, Manchester M14 7WN
Telephone Number: (061) 226-5047
Car Parking: Street Parking and Local Schools
Coach Parking: Kipax Street Car Park
Nearest Railway Station: Manchester Piccadilly (2.5 miles)
Nearest Bus Station: Chorlton Street
Club Shop:
Opening Times: Weekdays 9.30-5.00 Matchdays 9.30-5.30
Telephone No.: (061) 226-4824
Postal Sales: Yes
Nearest Police Station: Platt Lane, Moss Side, Manchester
Police Force: Greater Manchester
Police Telephone No.: (061) 872-5050

GROUND INFORMATION

Away Supporters' Entrances: Turnstiles 55, 56, 56A & 56B (Kippax). Also turnstiles 27 & 28 (North Stand)
Away Supporters' Sections: North Stand (Seating) & Kippax Street Stand (Standing).
Family Facilities: Location of Stand: Limited due to redevelopment. Family Season Ticket holders rehoused in North Stand K & L blocks.

ADMISSION INFO (1992/93 PRICES)

Adult Standing: £7.00
Adult Seating: £10.00 - £11.00
Child Standing: £4.00
Child Seating: £10 - £11 (Until Family Stand rebuilt)
Programme Price: £1.20
FAX Number: (061) 227-9418

Note : The Platt Lane Family Stand has been demolished and is expected to be rebuilt by February 1993.

```
           KIPPAX STREET STAND
        ┌──────────────────────────┐
CLAREMONT ROAD          MAIN STAND     (PLATT LANE STAND)
NORTH STAND             MAINE ROAD     (UNDER REDEVELOPMENT)
```

Travelling Supporters Information:

Routes: From North & West: Take M61 & M63 exit junction 9 following signs to Manchester (A5103). Turn right at crossroads (2.75 miles) into Claremont Road. After 0.25 mile turn right into Maine Road; From South: Exit M6 junction 19 to A556 and M56 junction 3 following signs to Manchester (A1503) (then as North); From East: Exit M62 junction 17 and take A56 to A57(M) (Manchester Airport) signs. Then follow Birmingham signs to A5103 and turn left into Claremont Road (1.25 miles) (then as North).

MANCHESTER UNITED FC

Founded: 1878	**Record Attendance**: 76,962 (25/3/39)
Turned Professional: 1902	**Colours**: Shirts - Red
Limited Company: 1907	Shorts - White
Admitted to League: 1892	**Telephone No.**: (061) 872-1661
Former Name(s): Newton Heath LYR FC	**Ticket Information**: (061) 872-0199
(1878-1892); Newton Heath FC (1892-1902)	**Pitch Size**: 116 × 76yds
Nickname: 'Red Devils'	**Ground Capacity**: 34,266
Ground: Old Trafford, Warwick Road North,	**Seating Capacity**: 30,700
Manchester M16 0RA	(Stretford End closed for re-development)

GENERAL INFORMATION
Supporters Club Administrator:
Barry Moorhouse
Address: c/o Club
Telephone Number: (061) 872-5208
Car Parking: Lancashire Cricket Ground
(1,200 cars) & White City (900 cars)
Coach Parking: By Police Direction
Nearest Railway Station: At Ground
Nearest Bus Station: Aytoun Street,
Manchester
Club Shop:
Opening Times: Weekdays & Matchdays
9.30-5.00pm
Telephone No.: (061) 872-3398
Postal Sales: Yes
Nearest Police Station: Talbot Road,
Stretford (0.5 mile)
Police Force: Greater Manchester
Police Telephone No.: (061) 872-5050

GROUND INFORMATION
Away Supporters' Entrances: Turnstiles 94-98
Scoreboard End - See Note
Away Supporters' Sections: Scoreboard End
Family Facilities: **Location of Stand**:
CNR Railway Side & Old Trafford End
Capacity of Stand: 2,007

ADMISSION INFO (1992/93 PRICES)
Adult Standing: £8.00
Adult Seating: £12.00 or £14.00 (Members)
Child Standing: N/A
Child Seating: £6.00, £7.00 or £8.00 (Members)
Programme Price: £1.00
FAX Number: (061) 896-5502
Note : During redevelopment, members have priority
for tickets and visitors may be unable to gain admission

(CLOSED FOR REDEVELOPMENT)
STRETFORD END

UNITED ROAD STAND
NORTH STAND LOWER

WARWICK ROAD NORTH
OLD TRAFFORD END
(Away)

SOUTH STAND LOWER
RAILWAY   FAMILY
MAIN STAND   STAND

Travelling Supporters Information:
Routes: From North & West: Take M61 to M63 and exit junction 4 and follow Manchester signs (A5081).
Turn right (2.5 miles) into Warwick Road; From South: Exit M6 junction 19 take Stockport (A556) then
Altrincham (A56). From Altrincham follow Manchester signs. turn left into Warwick Road (6 miles); From
East: Exit M62 junction 17 then A56 to Manchester. Follow signs South then Chester (Chester Road), turn
right into Warwick Road (2 miles).

MANSFIELD TOWN FC

Founded: 1891
Turned Professional: 1910
Limited Company: 1910
Admitted to League: 1931
Former Name(s): Mansfield Wesleyans FC
(1891-1905)
Nickname: 'Stags'
Ground: Field Mill Ground, Quarry Lane,
Mansfield, Notts.

Record Attendance: 24,467 (10/1/53)
Colours: Shirts - Amber/Blue Trim
Shorts - Royal Blue/Amber Trim
Telephone No.: (0623) 23567
Ticket Information: (0623) 23567
Pitch Size: 115 × 72yds
Ground Capacity: 10,315
Seating Capacity: 3,448

GENERAL INFORMATION
Supporters Club Administrator:
Miss M.Brown
Address: 44 Portland Avenue, Annesley
Woodhouse, Nottinghamshire
Telephone Number: (0623) 754-1823
Car Parking: Large Car Park at Ground
Coach Parking: Adjacent
Nearest Railway Station: Mansfield Alfreton Parkway - 9 miles (no public transport)
Nearest Bus Station: Mansfield
Club Shop:
Opening Times: Weekdays & Matchdays
9.00-5.00
Telephone No.: (0623) 658070
Postal Sales: Yes
Nearest Police Station: Mansfield (0.25 mile)
Police Force: Nottinghamshire
Police Telephone No.: (0623) 22622

GROUND INFORMATION
Away Supporters' Entrances: Quarry Lane Turnstiles
Away Supporters' Sections: Quarry Lane End (Open)
Family Facilities: **Location of Stand**:
Chad Family Stand
Capacity of Stand: 1,130

ADMISSION INFO (1992/93 PRICES)
Adult Standing: £6.00
Adult Seating: £8.00 (£6.00 in Family Stand)
Child Standing: £3.00
Child Seating: £4.00 (£4.00 in Family Stand)
Programme Price: £1.00
FAX Number: (0623) 25014

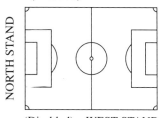

CHAD FAMILY STAND
(Disabled)

NORTH STAND

QUARRY LANE
(Away)

(Disabled)   WEST STAND

Travelling Supporters Information:
Routes: From North: Exit M1 junction 29, take A617 to Mansfield. After 6.25 miles turn right at Leisure Centre into Rosemary Street. Carry on to Quarry Lane and turn right; From South & West: Exit M1 junction 28, take A38 to Mansfield, after 6.5 miles turn right at crossroads into Belvedere Street, turn right after 0.25 mile into Quarry Lane; From East: Take A617 to Rainworth, turn right at crossroads (3 miles) into Windsor Road and turn right at end into Nottingham Road, then left into Quarry Lane.

MIDDLESBROUGH FC

Founded: 1876	**Record Attendance**: 53,596 (27/12/49)
Turned Professional: 1889	**Colours**: Shirts - Red with White Yoke
Limited Company: 1892	Shorts - White
Admitted to League: 1899	**Telephone No.**: (0642) 819659
Former Name(s): None	**Ticket Information**: (0642) 815996
Nickname: 'Boro'	**Pitch Size**: 114 × 73yds
Ground: Ayresome Park, Middlesbrough,	**Ground Capacity**: 26,101
Cleveland TS1 4PB	**Seating Capacity**: 12,585

GENERAL INFORMATION
Supporters Club Administrator:
Colin Haverson
Address: c/o Club
Telephone Number: (0642) 819659
Car Parking: Street Parking
Coach Parking: By Police Direction
Nearest Railway Station: Middlesbrough (1 mile)
Nearest Bus Station: Middlesbrough
Club Shop:
Opening Times: Monday-Friday 9.30-5.00 + Saturday Matchdays
Telephone No.: (0642) 826664
Postal Sales: Yes
Nearest Police Station: Dunning Street, Middlesbrough (1 mile)
Police Force: Cleveland
Police Telephone No.: (0642) 248184

GROUND INFORMATION
Away Supporters' Entrances: Turnstiles -South East Corner
Away Supporters' Sections: South East Corner (Open & Seating)
Family Facilities: **Location of Stand**:
North Stand
Capacity of Stand: 1,511

ADMISSION INFO (1992/93 PRICES)
Adult Standing: £8.00 (£6.00 in Family Group)
Adult Seating: £8.00 - £12.00
Child Standing: £3.00
Child Seating: £4.00
Programme Price: £1.00
FAX Number: (0642) 820244

```
                                    Disabled
        AYRESOME STREET             Section
          NORTH STAND
    ┌─────────────────────────┐
 W  H                         │  E (A
 E  O   ┌──┐           ┌──┐   │  A  Y
 S  L   │  │     ○     │  │   │  S  R
 T  G   └──┘           └──┘   │  T  E
 T  A                         │     S
 E  T                         │  S  O
 R  E                         │  T  M
 R  E                         │  A  E
 A  N                         │  N  P
 C  D   ┌──┐           ┌──┐   │  D  A
 E      │  │           │  │   │     R
        └──┘           └──┘   │     K
    └─────────────────────────┘
          SOUTH STAND                ROAD)
          CLIVE ROAD
                              South-East
                              Corner (Away)
```

Travelling Supporters Information:
Routes: From North: Take A19 across Tees Bridge and join A66 (0.25 mile). Take 3rd exit at roundabout (0.5 mile) into Heywood Street, and left into Ayresome Street at end; From South: Take A1 & A19 to junction with A66, take 4th exit at roundabout (0.5 mile) into Heywood Street (then as North); From West: Take A66 then 1.5 miles after Teesside Park Racecourse take 4th exit at roundabout into Ayresome Street.

MILLWALL FC

Founded: 1885
Turned Professional: 1893
Limited Company: 1894
Admitted to League: 1920
Former Name(s): Millwall Rovers FC (1885-1893) Millwall Athletic FC (1893-1925)
Nickname: 'Lions'
Ground: The Den, Cold Blow Lane, New Cross, London SE14 5RH

Record Attendance: 48,672 (20/2/37)
Colours: Shirts - Blue
          Shorts - White
Telephone No.: (071) 639-3143
Ticket Information: (071) 639-3143
Pitch Size: 112 × 74yds
Ground Capacity: 19,922
Seating Capacity: 2,690

GENERAL INFORMATION
Supporters Club Administrator: None
Address: -
Telephone Number: -
Car Parking: Ilderton Road Car Park
Coach Parking: Ilderton Road
Nearest Railway Station: New Cross Gate (0.5 mile)
Nearest Tube Station: New Cross Gate (0.5 mile)
Club Shop:
Opening Times: Daily 9.00-5.00
Telephone No.: (071) 358-0181
Postal Sales: Yes
Nearest Police Station: Deptford/Lewisham (1 mile)
Police Force: Metropolitan
Police Telephone No.: (071) 679-9217

GROUND INFORMATION
Away Supporters' Entrances: Ilderton Road (away fans must buy tickets from their own club) - Seating
Away Supporters' Sections: Ilderton Road End (Covered)
Family Facilities: **Location of Stand**: North Stand
Capacity of Stand: -

ADMISSION INFO (1991/92 PRICES)
Adult Standing: £7.00
Adult Seating: £9.20 - £11.00
Child Standing: £7.00
Child Seating: £9.20 - £11.00
Programme Price: £1.30
FAX Number: (071) 732-8075

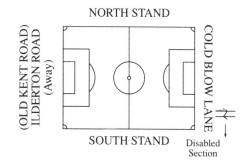

Travelling Supporters Information:
Routes: From North: Follow City signs from M1/A1 then signs for Shoreditch and Whitechapel. Follow signs Ring Road, Dover, cross over Tower Bridge, take 1st exit at roundabout (1 mile) onto A2. From Elephant & Castle take A2 (New Kent Road) into Old Kent Road and turn left (after 4 miles) at Canterbury Arms Pub into Ilderton Road (car park on right). Do not take routes into Cold Blow Lane; From South: Take A20 and A21 following signs to London. At New Cross follow signs for City, Westminster into Kender Street and follow into Avonley Road (then as North); From East: Take A2 to New Cross (then as South); From West: From M4 and M3 follow South Circular (A205) following signs for Clapham, City A3 then Camberwell, New Cross and then Rochester (A202). In 0.75 mile turn left into Kender Street (then as South).

NEWCASTLE UNITED FC

Founded: 1882	**Record Attendance**: 68,386 (3/9/30)
Turned Professional: 1889	**Colours**: Shirts - Black and White Stripes
Limited Company: 1890	Shorts - Black
Admitted to League: 1893	**Telephone No.**: (091) 232-8361
Former Name(s): Newcastle East End FC	**Ticket Information**: (091) 261-1571
(1882-92) Became 'United' when amalgamated	**Pitch Size**: 115 × 75yds
with Newcastle West End FC	**Ground Capacity**: 30,348
Nickname: 'Magpies'	**Seating Capacity**: 11,725

Ground: St.James Park, Newcastle-Upon-Tyne NE1 4ST

GENERAL INFORMATION
Supporters Club Administrator:
Kenneth Mullen
Address: 7 Prudhoe Place, Haymarket,
Newcastle-Upon-Tyne
Telephone Number: (091) 232-2473
Car Parking: Leazes Car Park & Street
Coach Parking: Leazes Car Park
Nearest Railway Station: Newcastle Central
(0.5 mile)
Nearest Bus Station: Gallowgate (0.25 mile)
Club Shop:
Opening Times: Monday-Saturday 9.00-5.00
Matchdays 9.00-5.30
Telephone No.: (091) 261-6357
Postal Sales: Yes
Also in MetroCentre, Gateshead, Monday-
Saturday 10.00-8.00 **Phone**: (091) 461-0000
Nearest Police Station: Market Street,
Newcastle
Police Force: Northumbria
Police Telephone No.: (091) 232-3451

GROUND INFORMATION
Away Supporters' Entrances: Turnstiles 45 & 46
Away Supporters' Sections: Leazes End 'H' Paddock
(Open)
Family Facilities: **Location of Stand**:
East Stand Paddock (seats) (Members only)
Capacity of Stand: 764 seated

ADMISSION INFO (1992/93 PRICES)
Adult Standing: £7.00
Adult Seating: £8.50 - £12.50. Family Enclosure £7
Child Standing: £3.50
Child Seating: £6.50 - £8.50 Family Enclosure £3.50
Programme Price: £1.00
FAX Number: (091) 232-9875

```
                ST. JAMES STREET
                   EAST STAND

 CAR PARK   ┌────────────────────┐  STRAWBERRY PLACE
 LEAZES END │    │          │    │  GALLOWGATE END
 (Away)     │    └──────────┘    │
            │         ○          │
            │    ┌──────────┐    │
            │    │          │    │
            └────────────────────┘
                MILBURN STAND
         BARRACK ROAD ⇄ BUS →
```

Travelling Supporters Information:
Routes: From North: Follow A1 into Newcastle, then Hexham signs into Percy Street. Turn right into Leazes Park Road; From South: Take A1M, then after Birtley Granada Services take A69 Gateshead Western
Bypass (bear left on Motorway). Follow Airport signs for approximately 3 miles then take A692 (Newcastle)
sign, crossing the Redheugh Bridge. At roundabout take 3rd exit (Blenheim Street). Proceed over two sets of
traffic lights crossing Westmorland Road and Westgate Road. Turn left into Bath Lane. Over traffic lights to
next roundabout and take third exit into Barrack Road; From West: Take A69 towards City Centre. Pass
Newcastle General Hospital. At traffic lights immediately after Hospital turn left into Brighton Grove and
after 70 yards turn right into Stanhope Street. Proceed into Barrack Road.

NORTHAMPTON TOWN FC

Founded: 1897	**Record Attendance**: 24,523 (23/4/66)
Turned Professional: 1901	**Colours**: Shirts - White with Claret Trim
Limited Company: 1901	Shorts - White with Claret Trim
Admitted to League: 1920	**Telephone No.**: (0604) 234100
Former Name(s): None	**Ticket Information**: (0604) 234100
Nickname: 'Cobblers'	**Pitch Size**: 112 × 75yds
Ground: County Ground, Abingdon Avenue,	**Ground Capacity**: 9,443
Northampton NN1 4PS	**Seating Capacity**: 360

GENERAL INFORMATION
Supporters Club Administrator:
Alec Smith
Address: c/o Club
Telephone Number: (0604) 842636
Car Parking: Street Parking
Coach Parking: Abingdon Park
Nearest Railway Station: Northampton
Castle
Nearest Bus Station: Greyfriars
Club Shop:
Opening Times: Weekdays - Office Hours
Matchdays 9.30-5.00
Telephone No.: (0604) 234100
Postal Sales: Yes
Nearest Police Station: Cambell Square,
Northampton
Police Force: Northants
Police Telephone No.: (0604) 33221

GROUND INFORMATION
Away Supporters' Entrances: Abingdon Avenue
Away Supporters' Sections: Spion Kop
Family Facilities: **Location of Stand**:
Abingdon Avenue Side
Capacity of Stand: 360

ADMISSION INFO (1992/93 PRICES)
Adult Standing: £5.00
Adult Seating: £7.50
Child Standing: £3.50
Child Seating: £7.50
Programme Price: £1.00
FAX Number: (0604) 604176

(CRICKET PITCH SIDE)
WANTAGE ROAD

SPION KOP (Away) — HOTEL END

(Away)
ABINGDON AVENUE

Travelling Supporters Information:
Routes: From North & West: Take A45 into Northampton and follow signs for Kettering (A43) into Kettering Road. After almost 1 mile turn right into Abingdon Avenue; From East: Take A45 to Wilby. After 5.25 miles continue across roundabout and in 2.5 miles turn right over crossroads into Abingdon Avenue; From South: Exit M1 junction 15 following signs for Kettering (A43) into Kettering Road (then as North).

NORWICH CITY FC

Founded: 1905	**Record Attendance**: 43,984 (30/3/63)
Turned Professional: 1905	**Colours**: Shirts - Yellow
Limited Company: 1905	Shorts - Green
Admitted to League: 1920	**Telephone No.**: (0603) 612131
Former Name(s): None	**Ticket Information**: (0603) 761661
Nickname: 'Canaries'	**Pitch Size**: 114 × 74yds
Ground: Carrow Road, Norwich NR1 1JE	**Ground Capacity**: 20,559
(Information Line (0603) 121514)	**Seating Capacity**: 20,559

GENERAL INFORMATION
Supporters Club Administrator:
Kevan Platt
Address: Club Canary, Carrow Road, Norwich
Telephone Number: (0603) 761125
Car Parking: City Centre Car Parks (nearby)
Coach Parking: Lower Clarence Road
Nearest Railway Station: Norwich (0.5 mile)
Nearest Bus Station: Surrey Street, Norwich
Club Shop: (In City Stand)
Opening Times: Weekdays & Matchdays
9.00-5.30pm
Telephone No.: (0603) 761125
Postal Sales: Yes
Nearest Police Station: Bethel Street,
Norwich (1 mile)
Police Force: Norfolk
Police Telephone No.: (0603) 621212

GROUND INFORMATION
Away Supporters' Entrances: Turnstiles 1-3 (Until
December 1992 - See Note)
Away Supporters' Sections: South Stand (Covered)
Family Facilities: **Location of Stand**:
South Stand
Capacity of Stand: 1,630

ADMISSION INFO (1992/93 PRICES)
Adult Standing: N/A
Adult Seating: £6.00 - £18.00
Child Standing: N/A
Child Seating: £3.00 - £9.00
Programme Price: £1.20
FAX Number: (0603) 665510
Note : The Barclay Stand (Carrow Road End) has been
demolished and should be rebuilt by December 1992
when away fans will be rehoused there. Prices vary
depending on opponents.

Travelling Supporters Information:
Routes: From North: Take A140 to junction with Ring Road and follow signs Yarmouth (A47) after 3.5
miles turn right at 'T' junction, turn left 0.5 mile into Carrow Road; From South & West: Take A11/A140
into Norwich and follow signs Yarmouth to Ring Road for Carrow Road; From East: Take A47 into Norwich then left onto Ring Road for Carrow Road.

NOTTINGHAM FOREST FC

Founded: 1865	**Record Attendance**: 49,945 (28/10/67)
Turned Professional: 1889	**Colours**: Shirts - Red
Limited Company: 1982	Shorts - White
Admitted to League: 1892	**Telephone No.**: (0602) 822202
Former Name(s): None	**Ticket Information**: (0602) 813801
Nickname: 'Reds' 'Forest'	**Pitch Size**: 115 × 78yds
Ground: City Ground, Nottingham	**Ground Capacity**: 31,091
NG2 5FJ	**Seating Capacity**: 15,114

GENERAL INFORMATION
Supporters Club Administrator:
Mr. B. Tewson
Address: c/o Club
Telephone Number: (0602) 822202
Car Parking: East Car Park (300 cars) &
Street Parking
Coach Parking: East Car Park, Meadow Lane
Nearest Railway Station: Nottingham
Midland (0.5 mile)
Nearest Bus Station: Victoria Street/
Broadmarsh Centre
Club Shop:
Opening Times: Weekdays 9.00-5.00
Matchdays 9.00-3.00
Telephone No.: (0602) 820444
Postal Sales: Yes
Nearest Police Station: Rectory Road, West
Bridgford (1 mile)
Police Force: Nottinghamshire
Police Telephone No.: (0602) 481888

GROUND INFORMATION
Away Supporters' Entrances: Via East Car Park
Away Supporters' Sections: T.Block Executive Stand
Family Facilities: Location of Stand:
Blocks G & Q Trent End
Capacity of Stand: -

ADMISSION INFO (1991/92 PRICES)
Adult Standing: £7.00
Adult Seating: £11.00 - £12.00
Child Standing: £5.00
Child Seating: £8.00 (Family Section Only)
Programme Price: £1.00
FAX Number: (0602) 455581
Note : A new 2-tier stand is being built at the Colwick
Road end - opening late 1992.

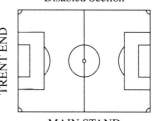

EXECUTIVE STAND (Away)
Disabled Section

RIVER TRENT / TRENT END

MAIN STAND / PAVILION ROAD

New Stand in Course of Construction - late 1992 / COLWICK ROAD

Travelling Supporters Information:
Routes: From North: Exit M1 junction 26 following Nottingham signs (A610) then Melton Mowbray and Trent Bridge (A606) signs. Cross River Trent, left into Radcliffe Road then left into Colwick Road; From South: Exit M1 junction 24 following signs Nottingham (South) to Trent Bridge. Turn right into Radcliffe Road then left into Colwick Road; From East: Take A52 to West Bridgford, turn right into Colwick Road; From West: Take A52 into Nottingham following signs Melton Mowbray and Trent Bridge, cross River Trent (then as North).

NOTTS COUNTY FC

Founded: 1862 (Oldest in League)	**Record Attendance**: 47,310 (12/3/55)
Turned Professional: 1885	**Colours**: Shirts - Black and White Stripes
Limited Company: 1888	Amber Sleeve & Trim
Admitted to League: 1888 (Founder)	Shorts - Black
Former Name(s): None	**Telephone No.**: (0602) 861155
Nickname: 'Magpies'	**Ticket Information**: (0602) 861155/850632
Ground: Meadow Lane, Nottingham	**Pitch Size**: 117 × 76yds
NG2 3HJ	**Ground Capacity**: 21,044
	Seating Capacity: 4,359

GENERAL INFORMATION
Supporters Club Administrator:
P. Dennis
Address: c/o Club
Telephone Number: (0602) 866802
Car Parking: British Waterways, Meadow Lane
Coach Parking: British Waterways
Nearest Railway Station: Nottingham Midland (0.5 mile)
Nearest Bus Station: Broadmarsh Centre
Club Shop:
Opening Times: Weekdays & Matchdays 9.00-5.00pm. Saturday non-matchdays 9-1pm
Telephone No.: (0602) 861155
Postal Sales: Yes
Nearest Police Station: Station Street, Nottingham
Police Force: Nottinghamshire
Police Telephone No.: (0602) 481888

GROUND INFORMATION
Away Supporters' Entrances: Cattle Market Corner, County Road
Away Supporters' Sections: Cattle Market Corner, County Road Stand (Some Covered)
Family Facilities: **Location of Stand**:
Meadow Lane End & Kop End Main Stand
Capacity of Stand: 2,260

ADMISSION INFO (1992/93 PRICES)
Adult Standing: £7.00
Adult Seating: £8.00 - £11.00
Child Standing: £5.00
Child Seating: £6.00 - £7.00
Programme Price: £1.20
FAX Number: (0602) 866442

COUNTY ROAD
(Away)   Disabled

CATTLE MARKET ROAD
SPION KOP

SPORTS CENTRE
MEADOW LANE

MAIN STAND

Travelling Supporters Information:
Routes: From North: Exit M1 junction 26 following Nottingham signs (A610) then Melton Mowbray and Trent Bridge (A606) signs. Before River Trent turn left into Meadow Lane; From South: Exit M1 junction 24 following signs Nottingham (South) to Trent Bridge, cross River and follow one-way system to the right, then turn left and right at traffic lights then second right into Meadow Lane; From East: Take A52 to West Bridgford/Trent Bridge, cross River and follow one-way system to the right then turn left and right at traffic lights, then second right into Meadow Lane; From West: Take A52 into Nottingham following signs Melton Mowbray and Trent Bridge, before River Trent turn left into Meadow Lane.

OLDHAM ATHLETIC FC

Founded: 1894	**Record Attendance**: 47,671 (25/1/30)
Turned Professional: 1899	**Colours**: Shirts - Blue
Limited Company: 1906	Shorts - Blue
Admitted to League: 1907	**Telephone No.**: (061) 624-4972 (24 hours)
Former Name(s): Pine Villa FC (1894-99)	**Ticket Information**: (061) 624-4972
Nickname: 'Latics'	**Pitch Size**: 110 × 74yds
Ground: Boundary Park, Oldham OL1 2PA	**Ground Capacity**: 16,700
	Seating Capacity: 11,100

GENERAL INFORMATION

Supporters Club Administrator:
Alan Hardy
Address: c/o Club
Telephone Number: (061) 627-1802
Car Parking: Lookers Stand Car Park
(1,000 cars)
Coach Parking: At Ground
Nearest Railway Station: Oldham Werneth
(1.5 miles)
Nearest Bus Station: Oldham Mumps
(2 miles)
Club Shop:
Opening Times: Mondays-Saturdays
9.00-5.00
Telephone No.: (061) 652-0966
Postal Sales: Yes
Nearest Police Station: Chadderton
Police Force: Greater Manchester
Police Telephone No.: (061) 624-0444

GROUND INFORMATION

Away Supporters' Entrances: Rochdale Road
Turnstiles and Turnstile 14 George Hill Stand
Away Supporters' Sections: Rochdale Road Stand
(seating)
Family Facilities: **Location of Stand**:
Lookers Stand
Capacity of Stand: 1,500

ADMISSION INFO (1992/93 PRICES)

Adult Standing: £7 Members £7.50 Non-members
Adult Seating: £9.50 - £12.00
Child Standing: £4.50
Child Seating: £6.00 - £7.50
Programme Price: £1.20
FAX Number: (061) 627-5915

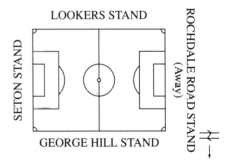

LOOKERS STAND

SETON STAND

ROCHDALE ROAD STAND
(Away)

GEORGE HILL STAND

Travelling Supporters Information:
Routes: From All Parts: Exit M62 junction 20 and take A627M to junction with A664. Take 1st exit at roundabout on to Broadway, then 1st right into Hilbre Avenue which leads to car park.

OXFORD UNITED FC

Founded: 1893
Turned Professional: 1949
Limited Company: 1949
Admitted to League: 1962
Former Name(s): Headington United FC
(1893-1960)
Nickname: 'U's'
Ground: Manor Ground, London Road,
Headington, Oxford   OX3 7RS

Record Attendance: 22,730 (29/2/64)
Colours: Shirts - Yellow with Navy Trim
　　　　　Shorts - Navy with Yellow Trim
Telephone No.: (0865) 61503
Ticket Information: (0865) 61503
Pitch Size: 110 × 75yds
Ground Capacity: 11,071
Seating Capacity: 2,777

GENERAL INFORMATION
Supporters Club Administrator:
Gary Whiting
Address: c/o Club
Telephone Number: (0865) 63063
Car Parking: Street Parking
Coach Parking: Headley Way
Nearest Railway Station: Oxford (3 miles)
Nearest Bus Station: Queen's Lane (2 miles)
Club Shop: 67 London Road, Headington
Opening Times: Monday-Saturday 9.30-5.30
(closes 3.00pm Matchdays)
Telephone No.: (0865) 61503
Postal Sales: Yes
Nearest Police Station: Cowley (2 miles)
Police Force: Thames Valley
Police Telephone No.: (0865) 777501

GROUND INFORMATION
Away Supporters' Entrances: Cuckoo Lane
Turnstiles 5-11
Away Supporters' Sections: Cuckoo Lane Stand
Family Facilities:　**Location of Stand:**
Beech Road Side (Members only)
Capacity of Stand: 162 uncovered seating,
170 covered seating

ADMISSION INFO (1991/92 PRICES)
Adult Standing: £7.00 (£6.00 members)
Adult Seating: £10.00
Child Standing: £4.50 (£3.00 members)
Child Seating: £5.00
Programme Price: £1.20
FAX Number: (0865) 741820

OSLER ROAD

CUCKOO LANE
(Away)

LONDON ROAD

Disabled　BEECH ROAD
Section

Travelling Supporters Information:
Routes: From North: Follow signs Ring Road, London (A40), take 4th exit at roundabout towards
Headington, turn right (0.75 mile) into Sandfield Road, then right into Beech Road; From South: Take A34
to bypass London (A4142), take 1st exit at roundabout towards Headington (then as North);
From East: Take M40 to A40, take 2nd exit at roundabout to Headington (then as North); From West: Take
A420 into Oxford and follow signs London along Headington Road, turn left (2 miles) into Sandfield Road,
then right into Beech Road.
Bus Services: Service 1 Railway Station to Queen's Lane, Service 2 to Ground.

PETERBOROUGH UNITED FC

Founded: 1923
Turned Professional: 1934
Limited Company: 1934
Admitted to League: 1960
Former Name(s): Peterborough & Fletton United FC (1923-34)
Nickname: 'Posh'
Ground: London Road, Peterborough, Cambs   PE2 8AL

Record Attendance: 30,096   (20/2/65)
Colours: Shirts - Blue
          Shorts - White
Telephone No.: (0733) 63947
Ticket Information: (0733) 63947
Pitch Size: 112 × 76yds
Ground Capacity: 16,414
Seating Capacity: 3,500

GENERAL INFORMATION
Supporters Club Administrator: Rob Scott
Address: c/o Club
Telephone Number: -
Car Parking: Ample Parking at Ground
Coach Parking: Rear of Ground
Nearest Railway Station: Peterborough (1 mile)
Nearest Bus Station: Peterborough (0.25 mile)
Club Shop:
Opening Times: Monday-Friday 9.00-5.00 (Closes for Lunch 1.00-2.00)
Telephone No.: (0733) 63947
Postal Sales: Yes
Nearest Police Station: Bridge Street, Peterborough (5 minutes walk)
Police Force: Cambridgeshire
Police Telephone No.: (0733) 63232

GROUND INFORMATION
Away Supporters' Entrances: Turnstile A, Moys End
Away Supporters' Sections: Moys End (Covered Standing) - Block A seating
Family Facilities: Location of Stand: Family Stand
Capacity of Stand: 3,500

ADMISSION INFO (1991/92 PRICES)
Adult Standing: £6.00
Adult Seating: £8.00
Child Standing: £3.50
Child Seating: £4.00
Programme Price: £1.00
FAX Number: (0733) 557210

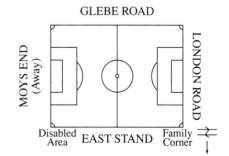

GLEBE ROAD

MOYS END (Away)

LONDON ROAD

Disabled Area   EAST STAND   Family Corner

Travelling Supporters Information:
Routes: From North & West: Take A1 then A47 into Town Centre, follow Whittlesey signs across river into London Road; From East: Take A47 into Town Centre (then as North); From South: Take A1 then A15 into London Road.

PLYMOUTH ARGYLE FC

Founded: 1886	**Record Attendance**: 43,596 (10/10/36)
Turned Professional: 1903	**Colours**: Shirts - Green & White Stripes
Limited Company: 1903	Shorts - Black
Admitted to League: 1920	**Telephone No.**: (0752) 562561
Former Name(s): Argyle FC (1886-1903)	**Ticket Information**: (0752) 562561
Nickname: 'Pilgrims' 'Argyle'	**Pitch Size**: 112 × 72yds
Ground: Home Park, Plymouth PL2 3DQ	**Ground Capacity**: 19,900
	Seating Capacity: 6,700

GENERAL INFORMATION
Supporters Club Administrator:
S. Rendell
Address: c/o Club
Telephone Number: (0752) 562561
Car Parking: Car Park (1,000 Cars) Adjacent
Coach Parking: Central Car Park
Nearest Railway Station: Plymouth North Road
Nearest Bus Station: Bretonside, Plymouth
Club Shop:
Opening Times: Monday-Saturday 9.00-5.00
Telephone No.: (0752) 558292
Postal Sales: Yes
Nearest Police Station: Devonport (1 mile)
Police Force: Devon & Cornwall
Police Telephone No.: (0752) 701188

GROUND INFORMATION
Away Supporters' Entrances: Barn Park End Turnstiles (standing)
Away Supporters' Sections: Barn Park End (Open)
Family Facilities: **Location of Stand**:
Devonport End of Grandstand
Capacity of Stand: 200

ADMISSION INFO (1992/93 PRICES)
Adult Standing: £5.50 or £6.00
Adult Seating: £8.00 - £10.00
Child Standing: £3.50
Child Seating: £6.00
Programme Price: £1.00
FAX Number: (0752) 606167
Note: There are special rates for adults & children in the Family Enclosure. OAPs may be charged a little more than children in some parts of the ground.

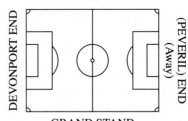

TAVISTOCK ROAD
LYNDHURST STAND

DEVONPORT END

BARN PARK (PEVERIL) END (Away)

GRAND STAND

Travelling Supporters Information:
Routes: From All Parts: Take A38 to Tavistock Road (A386), then branch left following signs Plymouth (A386), continue for 1.25 miles - car park on left.

PORTSMOUTH FC

Founded: 1898	**Record Attendance**: 51,385 (26/2/49)
Turned Professional: 1898	**Colours**: Shirts - Blue
Limited Company: 1898	Shorts - White
Admitted to League: 1920	**Telephone No.**: (0705) 731204
Former Name(s): None	**Ticket Information**: (0705) 750825
Nickname: 'Pompey'	**Pitch Size**: 115 × 73yds
Ground: Fratton Park, 57 Frogmore Road,	**Ground Capacity**: 26,300
Portsmouth, Hants PO4 8RA	**Seating Capacity**: 7,000

GENERAL INFORMATION
Supporters Club Administrator: -
Address: c/o Club
Telephone Number: -
Car Parking: Street Parking
Coach Parking: By Police Direction
Nearest Railway Station: Fratton (Adjacent)
Nearest Bus Station: Eastney
Club Shop:
Opening Times: Monday-Saturday 9.00-5.00
Telephone No.: (0705) 738358
Postal Sales: Yes
Nearest Police Station: Southsea
Police Force: Hampshire
Police Telephone No.: (0705) 321111

GROUND INFORMATION
Away Supporters' Entrances: Aspley Road - Milton Road side
Away Supporters' Sections: Aspley Road End (Open)
Family Facilities: Location of Stand:
2 - South Enclosure, Carisbrooke Road & 'G' Section, Milton Road
Capacity of Stand: 3,300 (S);   3,200 (N)

ADMISSION INFO (1992/93 PRICES)
Adult Standing: £7.00
Adult Seating: £10.00 - £14.00
Child Standing: £5.00
Child Seating: £6.00 - £7.00
Programme Price: £1.20
FAX Number: (0705) 734129

```
         MILTON ROAD
         NORTH STAND
FROGMORE ROAD  ┌──────────────┐  ASPLEY ROAD
FRATTON ROAD   │              │  (MILTON END)
(Disabled Section)│          │  (Away)
               └──────────────┘
         SOUTH STAND
         CARISBROOKE ROAD
```

Travelling Supporters Information:
Routes: From North & West: Take M27 and M275 to end then take 2nd exit at roundabout and in 0.25 mile turn right at 'T' junction into London Road (A2047), in 1.25 mile cross railway bridge and turn left into Goldsmith Avenue. After 0.5 mile turn left into Frogmore Road; From East: Take A27 following Southsea signs (A2030). Turn left at roundabout (3 miles) into A288, then right into Priory Crescent and next right into Carisbrooke Road

PORT VALE FC

Founded: 1876	**Record Attendance**: 50,000 (20/2/60)
Turned Professional: 1885	**Colours**: Shirts - White
Limited Company: 1911	Shorts - Black
Admitted to League: 1892	**Telephone No.**: (0782) 814134
Former Name(s): Burslem Port Vale FC	**Ticket Information**: (0782) 814134
(1876-1913)	**Pitch Size**: 114 × 77yds
Nickname: 'Valiants'	**Ground Capacity**: 21,662
Ground: Vale Park, Burslem, Stoke-on-Trent,	**Seating Capacity**: 12,442
ST6 1AW	

GENERAL INFORMATION
Supporters Club Administrator:
G. Wakefield
Address: c/o Club
Telephone Number: (0538) 266228
Car Parking: Car Parks at Ground
Coach Parking: Hamil Road Car Park
Nearest Railway Station: Longport, Stoke
Nearest Bus Station: Burslem
Adjacent
Club Shop:
Opening Times: Monday-Saturday 9.00-5.30
Telephone No.: (0782) 835524
Postal Sales: Yes
Nearest Police Station: Burslem
Police Force: Staffordshire
Police Telephone No.: (0782) 577114

GROUND INFORMATION
Away Supporters' Entrances: Hamil Road turnstiles
Away Supporters' Sections: Hamil Road End &
Railway Stand - Block C
Family Facilities: **Location of Stand**:
Railway Stand/Bycars Corner
Capacity of Stand: 1,000

ADMISSION INFO (1992/93 PRICES)
Adult Standing: £5.00 or £6.00 (Family Terrace)
Adult Seating: £6, £7, £8 or £9 (Family Stand)
Child Standing: £3.50 or £4.00 (Family Terrace)
Child Seating: £4, £5.50, £6 or £6.50 (Family Stand)
Programme Price: £1.00
FAX Number: (0782) 834981

Travelling Supporters Information:
Routes: From North: Exit M6 junction 16 and follow Stoke signs (A500). Branch left off the A500 at the exit signposted Tunstall and take 1st exit at roundabout onto A50. Turn right 0.25 mile into Newcastle Street and at end cross into Moorland Road. Then turn left into Hamil Road; From South & West: Exit M6 junction 15 and take A5006 and A500, after 6.25 miles branch left (then as North); From East: Take A50 or A52 into Stoke following Burslem signs into Waterloo Road, turn right at Burslem crossroads into Moorland Road (then as North).

PRESTON NORTH END FC

<table>
<tr><td>Founded: 1881</td><td>Record Attendance: 42,684 (23/4/38)</td></tr>
<tr><td>Turned Professional: 1885</td><td>Colours: Shirts - White</td></tr>
<tr><td>Limited Company: 1893</td><td>Shorts - Blue</td></tr>
<tr><td>Admitted to League: 1888</td><td>Telephone No.: (0772) 795919</td></tr>
<tr><td>Former Name(s): Preston Nelson FC (1881-2)</td><td>Ticket Information: (0772) 709170</td></tr>
<tr><td>Nickname: 'Lilywhites' 'North End'</td><td>Pitch Size: 110 × 72yds</td></tr>
<tr><td>Ground: Lowthorpe Road, Deepdale,</td><td>Ground Capacity: 16,500</td></tr>
<tr><td>Preston PR1 6RU</td><td>Seating Capacity: 3,000</td></tr>
</table>

GENERAL INFORMATION
Supporters Club Administrator:
Maureen Robinson
Address: 40 Southgate, Fulwood, Preston
Telephone Number: (0772) 774005
Car Parking: West Stand Car Park (600 cars)
Coach Parking: West Stand Car Park
Nearest Railway Station: Preston (2 miles)
Nearest Bus Station: Preston (1 mile)
Club Shop:
Opening Times: Weekdays 9.00-4.30
Matchdays 12.30-3.00
Telephone No.: (0772) 795465
Postal Sales: Yes
Nearest Police Station: Lawson Street,
Preston (1 mile)
Police Force: Lancashire
Police Telephone No.: (0772) 203203

GROUND INFORMATION
Away Supporters' Entrances: Turnstiles 3-11
Deepdale Road (Standing); Turnstiles 13-14 (Seats)
Away Supporters' Sections: Town End (Covered),
West Stand (Seats)
Family Facilities: **Location of Stand**:
West Stand
Capacity of Stand: 300

ADMISSION INFO (1992/93 PRICES)
Adult Standing: £5.50 or £6.00
Adult Seating: £7.00 or £8.00
Child Standing: £3.50 or £4.50
Child Seating: £5.00 or £6.00
Programme Price: £1.00
FAX Number: (0772) 653266

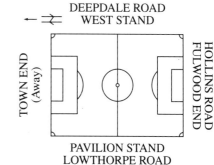

Travelling Supporters Information:
Routes: From North: M6 then M55 to junction 1. Follow signs to Preston A6. After 2 miles turn left at the crossroads into Blackpool Road (A5085). Turn right 0.75 mile into Deepdale; From South & East: Exit M6 junction 31 and follow Preston signs (A59). Take 2nd exit at roundabout (1 mile) into Blackpool Road. Turn left (1.25 mile) into Deepdale; From West: Exit M55 junction 1 (then as North).

QUEEN'S PARK RANGERS FC

Founded: 1882
Turned Professional: 1898
Limited Company: 1899
Admitted to League: 1920
Former Name(s): Formed by amalgamation of St. Jude's & Christchurch Rangers FC
Nickname: 'Rangers'   'R's'
Ground: Rangers Stadium, South Africa Road London   W12 7PA

Record Attendance: 35,353 (27/4/74)
Colours: Shirts - Blue and White Hoops Shorts - White
Telephone No.: (081) 743-0262
Ticket Information: (081) 749-5744
Pitch Size: 110 × 75yds
Ground Capacity: 23,480
Seating Capacity: 15,026

GENERAL INFORMATION

Supporters Club Administrator: Neil Roberts
Address: c/o Club
Telephone Number: (081) 749-6771
Car Parking: White City NCP
Coach Parking: White City
Nearest Railway Station: Shepherd's Bush
Nearest Tube Station: White City (Central)
Club Shop:
Opening Times: Monday-Saturday 9.00-5.00
Telephone No.: (081) 743-0262
Postal Sales: Yes
Nearest Police Station: Uxbridge Road, Shepherd's Bush (0.5 mile)
Police Force: Metropolitan
Police Telephone No.: (081) 741-6212

GROUND INFORMATION

Away Supporters' Entrances: South Africa Road, Turnstiles 29-34 & Ellerslie Road, Nºs 35-37
Away Supporters' Sections: West End Stand (Partially covered)
Family Facilities: Location of Stand: Loftus Road Stand
Capacity of Stand: 3,152 seating

ADMISSION INFO (1992/93 PRICES)

Adult Standing: £8.00 - £10.00
Adult Seating: £11.00 - £25.00
Child Standing: £5.00
Child Seating: £11.00 - £25.00
Programme Price: £1.30
FAX Number: (081) 749-0994
Note : Prices vary depending on opponents. No Child concessions for Category 'A' games

(Disabled)

ELLERSLIE ROAD STAND

LOFTUS ROAD STAND

WEST END STAND (SCHOOL) (Away)

BLOEMFONTEIN ROAD

MAIN STAND
SOUTH AFRICA ROAD

Travelling Supporters Information:
Routes: From North: Take M1 & A406 North Circular for Neasden, turn left 0.75 mile (A404) following signs Harlesden, then Hammersmith, past White City Stadium and right into White City Road, then left into South Africa Road; From South: Take A206, A3 across Putney Bridge following signs to Hammersmith, then Oxford A219 to Shepherd's Bush to join A4020 following signs to Acton, in 0.25 mile turn right into Loftus Road; From East: Take A12, A406 then A503 to join Ring Road follow Oxford signs to join A40(M), branch left (2 miles) to M41, 3rd exit at roundabout to A4020 (then as South); From West: Take M4 to Chiswick then A315 and A402 to Shepherd's Bush, join A4020 (then as South).

READING FC

Founded: 1871	**Record Attendance**: 33,042 (19/2/27)
Turned Professional: 1895	**Colours**: Shirts - Navy & White
Limited Company: 1897	Shorts - Navy
Admitted to League: 1920	**Telephone No.**: (0734) 507878
Former Name(s): Amalgamated with Hornets	**Ticket Information**: (0734) 507878
FC (1877) and Earley FC (1889)	**Pitch Size**: 112 × 77yds
Nickname: 'Royals'	**Ground Capacity**: 13,200
Ground: Elm Park, Norfolk Road, Reading,	**Seating Capacity**: 2,100
RG3 2EF	

GENERAL INFORMATION
Supporters Club Administrator: Mrs J. Hill
Address: c/o Club
Telephone Number: (0734) 507878
Car Parking: Street Parking
Coach Parking: The Meadway
Nearest Railway Station: Reading West
(0.5 mile)
Nearest Bus Station: Reading
Club Shop: Via Ticket Office
Opening Times: Monday-Friday &
Matchdays 9.00-5.00pm
Telephone No.: (0734) 507878
Postal Sales: Yes
Nearest Police Station: Castle Street,
Reading (2 miles)
Police Force: Thames Valley
Police Telephone No.: (0734) 536000

GROUND INFORMATION
Away Supporters' Entrances: Norfolk Road
Turnstiles
Away Supporters' Sections: Reading End/Norfolk
Road (Open Terrace) + 'A' Stand Seating
Family Facilities: Location of Stand:
Norfolk Road side 'E' Stand
Capacity of Stand: 299

ADMISSION INFO (1992/93 PRICES)
Adult Standing: £6.00
Adult Seating: £7.00 - £9.00
Child Standing: £3.00
Child Seating: £5.00 - £9.00
Programme Price: £1.20
FAX Number: (0734) 566628

TILEHURST ROAD
(SOUTH BANK)

SUFFOLK ROAD
READING END
(Away)

WANTAGE ROAD
TILEHURST END

NORFOLK ROAD

Travelling Supporters Information:
Routes: From North: Take A423, A4074 and A4155 from Oxford across railway bridge into Reading. Follow signs for Newbury (A4) into Castle Hill, then right into Tilehurst Road. Turn right after 0.75 mile into Cranbury Road then left and 2nd left into Norfolk Road; From South: Take A33 into Reading and follow Newbury signs into Bath Road. Cross railway bridge and take 3rd right into Liebenrood Road. At the end turn right into Tilehurst Road then 1st left into Cranbury Road and 2nd left into Norfolk Road; From East: Exit M4 junction 10 and use A329 and A4 into Reading. Cross railway bridge (then as South); From West: Exit M4 junction 12 and take A4. After 3.25 miles turn left into Liebenrood Road (then as South).

ROCHDALE FC

Founded: 1907
Turned Professional: 1907
Limited Company: 1910
Admitted to League: 1921
Former Name(s): Rochdale Town FC
Nickname: 'The Dale'
Ground: Willbutts Lane, Spotland, Rochdale OL11 5DS

Record Attendance: 24,231 (10/12/49)
Colours: Shirts - Blue & White
Shorts - Blue & White
Telephone No.: (0706) 44648
Ticket Information: (0706) 44649
Pitch Size: 111 × 77yds
Ground Capacity: 10,735
Seating Capacity: 642 - See Note

GENERAL INFORMATION
Supporters Club Administrator:
R.I. Bailey
Address: c/o Club
Telephone Number: -
Car Parking: Car Park at Ground
Coach Parking: Rear of Pearl Street Stand
Nearest Railway Station: Rochdale (1.5 mls)
Nearest Bus Station: Town Centre (1 mile)
Club Shop:
Opening Times: Matchdays Only
Telephone No.: (0706) 44648
Postal Sales: Yes
Nearest Police Station: Rochdale (1.5 miles)
Police Force: Greater Manchester
Police Telephone No.: (0706) 47401

GROUND INFORMATION
Away Supporters' Entrances: Pearl Street Turnstiles
Away Supporters' Sections: Pearl St. End (Open & Covered)
Family Facilities: Location of Stand:
'B' Stand
Capacity of Stand: 120

ADMISSION INFO (1992/93 PRICES)
Adult Standing: £5.00
Adult Seating: N/A until December 1992
Child Standing: £2.50
Child Seating: N/A until December 1992
Programme Price: £1.00
FAX Number: (0706) 48466
Note : The Main Stand has been demolished and is to be rebuilt by December 1992. Seating and capacity are not yet available.

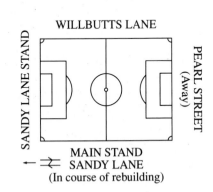

WILLBUTTS LANE

SANDY LANE STAND

PEARL STREET
(Away)

MAIN STAND
SANDY LANE
(In course of rebuilding)

Travelling Supporters Information:
Routes: From North: Take A680 to Rochdale, watch out for right turn into Willbutts Lane; From South, East & West: Exit M62 junction 20 following Rochdale signs, take 2nd exit at 2nd roundabout (1.5 miles) into Roch Valley Way and turn right (1.5 miles) into Willbutts Lane.

ROTHERHAM UNITED FC

Founded: 1884
Turned Professional: 1905
Limited Company: 1920
Admitted to League: 1893
Former Name(s): Thornhill United FC (1884-1905); Rotherham County FC (1905-1925)
Nickname: 'The Merry Millers'
Ground: Millmoor Ground, Rotherham S60 1HR

Record Attendance: 25,000 (13/12/52)
Colours: Shirts - Red
Shorts - White
Telephone No.: (0709) 562434
Ticket Information: (0709) 562434
Pitch Size: 115 × 76yds
Ground Capacity: 14,000
Seating Capacity: 3,407

GENERAL INFORMATION

Supporters Club Administrator:
Mrs R. Cowley
Address: 50 Lister Street, Rotherham
Telephone Number: (0709) 375831
Car Parking: Kimberworth Road and Main Street Car Parks
Coach Parking: By Police Direction
Nearest Railway Station: Rotherham Central (0.5 mile)
Nearest Bus Station: Town Centre (0.5 mile)
Club Shop:
Opening Times: Monday-Saturday 9.00-5.00
Telephone No.: (0709) 562760
Postal Sales: Yes
Nearest Police Station: Rotherham (0.5 mile)
Police Force: South Yorkshire
Police Telephone No.: (0709) 371121

GROUND INFORMATION

Away Supporters' Entrances: Millmoor Lane Turnstiles
Away Supporters' Sections: Millmoor Lane/Railway End
Family Facilities: **Location of Stand**: Millmoor Lane Side
Capacity of Stand: 748

ADMISSION INFO (1992/93 PRICES)

Adult Standing: £5.00
Adult Seating: £6.00 - £7.50
Child Standing: £3.80
Child Seating: £4.50 - £5.50
Programme Price: £1.00
FAX Number: (0709) 563336

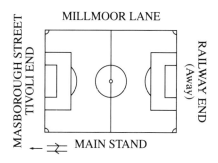

Travelling Supporters Information:
Routes: From North: Exit M1 junction 34 following Rotherham (A6109) signs to traffic lights and turn right into Millmoor Lane. Ground is 0.24 mile on right over railway bridge; From South & West: Exit M1 junction 33, turn right following 'Rotherham' signs. Turn left at roundabout and right at next roundabout. Follow dual carriageway to next roundabout and go straight on. Turn left at next roundabout and ground is 0.25 mile on left; From East: Take A630 into Rotherham following Sheffield signs. At 2nd roundabout turn right into Masborough Street then 1st left into Millmoor Lane.

SCARBOROUGH FC

<table>
<tr><td>

Founded: 1879
Limited Company: 1933
Admitted to League: 1987
Former Name(s): None
Nickname: 'Boro'
Ground: McCain Stadium, Seamer Road, Scarborough, N.Yorks

</td><td>

Record Attendance: 11,124 (1938)
Colours: Shirts - Red
          Shorts - White
Telephone No.: (0723) 375094
Ticket Information: (0723) 375094
Pitch Size: 112 × 74yds
Ground Capacity: 10,000
Seating Capacity: 864

</td></tr>
</table>

GENERAL INFORMATION
Social Club Administrator: Helen Crinnion
Address: c/o Club
Telephone Number: (0723) 375094
Car Parking: Street Parking
Coach Parking: At Ground
Nearest Railway Station: Scarborough Central (2 miles)
Nearest Bus Station: Westwood Scarborough (2 miles)
Club Shop:
Opening Times: Weekdays 9.30-5.00pm & Matchdays
Telephone No.: (0723) 375094
Postal Sales: Yes
Nearest Police Station: Scarborough (2 mls)
Police Force: North Yorkshire
Police Telephone No.: (0723) 363333

GROUND INFORMATION
Away Supporters' Entrances: Edgehill Road Turnstiles
Away Supporters' Sections: Visitors Enclosure, Edgehill Road End
Family Facilities: **Location of Stand**: To right of Main Stand
Capacity of Stand: 200 Standing

ADMISSION INFO (1992/93 PRICES)
Adult Standing: £6.00
Adult Seating: £8.50
Child Standing: £3.00
Child Seating: £5.50
Programme Price: 90p
FAX Number: (0723) 378733

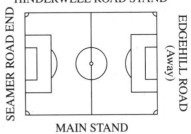

Travelling Supporters Information:
Routes: The Ground is situated on the main York to Scarborough Road (A64) 0.5 mile on left past B & Q DIY Store.

SCUNTHORPE UNITED FC

Founded: 1899	**Record Attendance**: 8,775 (1/5/89)
Turned Professional: 1912	**Colours**: Shirts - Sky Blue with Claret trim
Limited Company: 1912	Shorts - Sky Blue
Admitted to League: 1950	**Telephone No.**: (0724) 848077
Former Name(s): Scunthorpe & Lindsey	**Ticket Information**: (0724) 848077
United (1899-1912)	**Pitch Size**: 111 × 73yds
Nickname: 'Irons'	**Ground Capacity**: 9,200
Ground: Glanford Park, Doncaster Road,	**Seating Capacity**: 6,400
Scunthorpe, South Humberside DN15 8TD	

GENERAL INFORMATION
Supporters Club Administrator:
Ian Burton
Address: 5 Chatman Avenue, Scunthorpe
Telephone Number: -
Car Parking: For 600 cars at Ground
Coach Parking: At Ground
Nearest Railway Station: Scunthorpe
(1.5 miles)
Nearest Bus Station: Scunthorpe (1.5 miles)
Club Shop:
Opening Times: Weekdays & Matchdays
9.00-5.00
Telephone No.: (0724) 848077
Postal Sales: Yes
Nearest Police Station: Laneham Street,
Scunthorpe (1.5 miles)
Police Force: Humberside
Police Telephone No.: (0724) 843434

GROUND INFORMATION
Away Supporters' Entrances: Turnstiles 6-7
Away Supporters' Sections: South Stand
Family Facilities: **Location of Stand**:
Clugston Stand
Capacity of Stand: 2,277

ADMISSION INFO (1992/93 PRICES)
Adult Standing: £5.00
Adult Seating: £6.50 - £7.50
Child Standing: £2.70
Child Seating: £3.30 or £5.00
Programme Price: £1.00
FAX Number: (0724) 857986

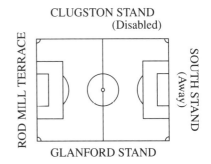

Travelling Supporters Information:
Routes: From All Parts: Exit M180 junction 3 onto M181. Follow M181 to roundabout with A18 and take A18 towards Scunthorpe - Ground on right.

SHEFFIELD UNITED FC

Founded: 1889
Turned Professional: 1889
Limited Company: 1899
Admitted to League: 1892
Former Name(s): None
Nickname: 'Blades'
Ground: Bramall Lane, Sheffield   S2 4SU

Record Attendance: 68,287 (15/2/36)
Colours: Shirts - Red & White Stripes with
Black Pinstripe
Shorts - Black
Telephone No.: (0742) 738955
Ticket Information: (0742) 738955
Pitch Size: 113 × 72yds
Ground Capacity: 32,893
Seating Capacity: 23,544

GENERAL INFORMATION

Supporters Club Administrator:
Beryl Whitney
Address: 42 Base Green Avenue, Sheffield
S12 3FA
Telephone Number: (0742) 390202
Car Parking: Street Parking
Coach Parking: By Police Direction
Nearest Railway Station: Sheffield Midland
(1 mile)
Nearest Bus Station: Pond Street, Sheffield
Club Shop:
Opening Times: Monday-Friday 9.30-5.00
Matchdays 9.30-5.30
Telephone No.: (0742) 750596
Postal Sales: Yes
Nearest Police Station: Police Room at
Ground
Police Force: South Yorkshire
Police Telephone No.: (0742) 768522

GROUND INFORMATION

Away Supporters' Entrances: Bramall Lane
Turnstiles
Away Supporters' Sections: Bramall Lane Stand &
Terrace (Mostly Covered)
Family Facilities: **Location of Stand**:
New South Stand - West Wing - Membership Area
Capacity of Stand: 2,500 (Family Section)

ADMISSION INFO (1992/93 PRICES)

Adult Standing: £7.00 'B'   £8.50 'A'
Adult Seating: £8 - £12.00 'B'   £9.00 - £14.00 'A'
Child Standing: £4.50 'B'   £5.00 'A'
Child Seating: £5.00 - £6.50 'B'   £6.00 - £7.00 'A'
Programme Price: £1.20
FAX Number: (0742) 723030
Note: Category 'A' games are more expensive than
those of 'B'. Prices are cheaper in the Family Enclosure - Members Only

CHERRY STREET
NEW SOUTH STAND

SHOREHAM STREET

SPION KOP

BRAMALL LANE
(Away)

JOHN STREET

Travelling Supporters Information:
Routes: From North: Exit M1 junction 34 following signs to Sheffield (A6109), turn left 3.5 miles and take
4th exit at roundabout into Sheaf Street. Take 5th exit at 2nd roundabout into St. Mary's Road (for Bakewell),
turn left 0.5 mile into Bramall Lane; From South & East: Exit M1 junctions 31 or 33 and take A57 to roundabout, take 3rd exit into Sheaf Street (then as North); From West: Take A57 into Sheffield and take 4th exit
at roundabout into Upper Hanover Street and at 2nd roundabout take 3rd exit into Bramall Lane.

SHEFFIELD WEDNESDAY FC

Founded: 1867
Turned Professional: 1887
Limited Company: 1899
Admitted to League: 1892
Former Name(s): The Wednesday FC
Nickname: 'Owls'
Ground: Hillsborough, Sheffield   S6 1SW

Record Attendance: 72,841 (17/2/34)
Colours: Shirts - Blue & White Stripes
Shorts - Black
Telephone No.: (0742) 343122
Ticket Information: (0742) 337233
Pitch Size: 115 × 75yds
Ground Capacity: 41,237
Seating Capacity: 23,370

GENERAL INFORMATION
Supporters Club Administrator:
Mrs Nettleship
Address: c/o Club
Telephone Number: (0742) 333419
Car Parking: Street Parking
Coach Parking: Owlerton Stadium
Nearest Railway Station: Sheffield (4 miles)
Nearest Bus Station: Sheffield (4 miles)
Club Shop:
Opening Times: Monday-Saturday
10.00-4.30
Telephone No.: (0742) 343342
Postal Sales: Yes
Nearest Police Station: Hammerton Road,
Sheffield (1 mile)
Police Force: South Yorkshire
Police Telephone No.: (0742) 343131

GROUND INFORMATION
Away Supporters' Entrances: West Stand Turnstiles
Away Supporters' Sections: West Stand
Family Facilities: Location of Stand:
Penistone Road Wing
Capacity of Stand: Approximately 1,000
ADMISSION INFO (1992/93 PRICES)
Adult Standing: £9.00
Adult Seating: £12.00 - £14.00
Child Standing: £4.50 - £6.50
Child Seating: £8.00 - £10.00
Programme Price: £1.20
FAX Number: (0742) 337145

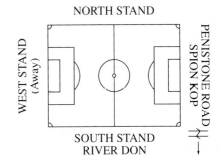

Travelling Supporters Information:
Routes: From North: Exit M1 junction 34 following signs for Sheffield (A6109), take 3rd exit (1.5 miles) at roundabout and in 3.25 miles turn left into Herries Road for Ground; From South & East: Exit M1 junctions 31 or 33 and take A57 to roundabout, take exit into Prince of Wales Road after 5.75 miles turn left into Herries Road South; From West: Take A57 until A6101 and turn left. After 3.75 miles turn left at 'T' junction into Penistone Road for Ground.

SHREWSBURY TOWN FC

Founded: 1886	**Record Attendance**: 18,917 (26/4/61)
Turned Professional: 1905	**Colours**: Shirts - Blue, Yellow & White
Limited Company: 1936	Shorts - Blue, Yellow & White
Admitted to League: 1950	**Telephone No.**: (0743) 360111
Former Name(s): None	**Ticket Information**: (0743) 360111
Nickname: 'Town' 'Shrews'	**Pitch Size**: 116 × 75yds
Ground: Gay Meadow, Shrewsbury	**Ground Capacity**: 15,000
SY2 6AB	**Seating Capacity**: 4,500

GENERAL INFORMATION
Supporters Club Administrator:
Fred Brown
Address: c/o Club
Telephone Number: (0743) 360111
Car Parking: Car Park Adjacent
Coach Parking: Gay Meadow
Nearest Railway Station: Shrewsbury
(1 mile)
Nearest Bus Station: Baker Street,
Shrewsbury
Club Shop:
Opening Times: Matchdays & Office Hours
Telephone No.: (0743) 356316
Postal Sales: Yes
Nearest Police Station: Clive Road,
Shrewsbury
Police Force: West Mercia
Police Telephone No.: (0743) 232888

GROUND INFORMATION
Away Supporters' Entrances: Station End Turnstiles
Away Supporters' Sections: Station Stand (Covered)
Family Facilities: **Location of Stand**:
Station Stand Side
Capacity of Stand: 500

ADMISSION INFO (1992/93 PRICES)
Adult Standing: £5.00
Adult Seating: £6.00 - £7.00
Child Standing: £3.00 or £5.00 for away fans
Child Seating: £4.00 - £7.00
Programme Price: 80p
FAX Number: (0743) 236384

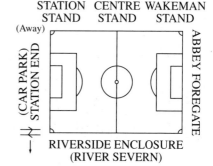

Travelling Supporters Information:
Routes: From North: Take A49 or A53 then 2nd exit at roundabout into Telford Way (A5112). After 0.75 mile take 2nd exit at roundabout. Turn right at 'T' junction into Abbey Foregate for Ground;
From South: Take A49 to Town Centre and at end of Coleham Head, turn right into Abbey Foregate;
From East: Take A5 then A458 into Town Centre straight forward to Abbey Foregate; From West: Take A458 then A5 around Ring Road, Roman Road, then turn left into Hereford Road and at end of Coleman Head turn right into Abbey Foregate.

SOUTHAMPTON FC

Founded: 1885
Turned Professional: 1894
Limited Company: 1897
Admitted to League: 1920
Former Name(s): Southampton St. Mary's YMCA FC (1885-1897)
Nickname: 'Saints'
Ground: The Dell, Milton Road, Southampton SO9 4XX

Record Attendance: 31,044 (8/10/69)
Colours: Shirts - Red & White
Shorts - Black
Telephone No.: (0703) 220505
Ticket Information: (0703) 228575
Pitch Size: 110 × 72yds
Ground Capacity: 21,919
Seating Capacity: 8,700

GENERAL INFORMATION
Supporters Club Administrator:
The Secretary
Address: Saints Supporters' Social Club, The Dell, Milton Road, Southampton
Telephone Number: -
Car Parking: Street Parking
Coach Parking: By Police Direction
Nearest Railway Station: Southampton Central (1 mile)
Nearest Bus Station: West Qua·· Road by Centre 2000
Club Shop:
Opening Times: Monday-Saturday 9.00-5.00
Telephone No.: (0703) 220505
Postal Sales: Yes
Nearest Police Station: Civic Centre, Southampton (1 mile)
Police Force: Hampshire
Police Telephone No.: (0703) 581111

GROUND INFORMATION
Away Supporters' Entrances: Archers Road Turnstiles
Away Supporters' Sections: Visitors enclosure Archers Road End (Open)
Family Facilities: Location of Stand:
Elevated Terrace - Milton Road
Capacity of Stand: 2,876

ADMISSION INFO (1992/93 PRICES)
Adult Standing: £7.00/£8.00
Adult Seating: £8.00 - £11.50/£10.00 - £14.00
Child Standing: £2.00
Child Seating: Same prices as adults
Programme Price: £1.00
FAX Number: (0703) 330360
Note: Matches are split into Categories of 'Silver' and 'Gold'. Prices shown to the left of the / are Silver

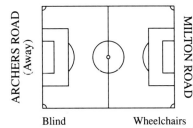

EAST STAND

ARCHERS ROAD (Away)

WILTON AVENUE MILTON ROAD

Blind   Wheelchairs
WEST STAND
HILL LANE/MILTON ROAD

Travelling Supporters Information:
Routes: From North: Take A33 into the Avenue and turn right into Northlands Road. Turn right at end into Archer's Road; From East: Take M27 to A334 and follow signs Southampton A3024. Then follow signs The West into Commercial Road, turn right into Hill Lane then 1st right into Milton Road; From West: Take A35 then A3024 following signs City Centre into Fourposts Hill then left into Hill Lane and 1st right into Milton Road.

SOUTHEND UNITED FC

Founded: 1906
Turned Professional: 1906
Limited Company: 1919
Admitted to League: 1920
Former Name(s): Southend Athletic FC
Nickname: 'Shrimpers' 'Blues'
Ground: Roots Hall Ground, Victoria Avenue,
Southend-on-Sea SS2 6NQ

Record Attendance: 31,033 (10/1/79)
Colours: Shirts - Blue with Yellow Trim
Shorts - Yellow
Telephone No.: (0702) 340707
Ticket Information: (0702) 435602
Pitch Size: 110 × 74yds
Ground Capacity: 13,598
Seating Capacity: 6,124

GENERAL INFORMATION
Supporters Club Secretary: Tony Walters
Address: c/o Club
Telephone Number: (0702) 342707
Car Parking: Car Park at Ground (500 cars)
- Season Ticket Holders Only + Street Parking
Coach Parking: Car Park
Nearest Railway Station: Prittlewell (0.5 ml)
Nearest Bus Station: London Road,
Southend
Club Shop:
Opening Times: Weekdays & Matchdays
10.30-4.30pm (except Wednesdays)
Telephone No.: (0702) 435067
Postal Sales: Yes
Nearest Police Station: Southend-on-Sea
(0.25 mile)
Police Force: Essex
Police Telephone No.: (0702) 431212

GROUND INFORMATION
Away Supporters' Entrances: East Stand Turnstiles
Away Supporters' Sections: South Bank Terrace
(Open);   East Stand South Seats
Family Facilities: Location of Stand:
East Stand + West Stand
Capacity of Stand: 2,2634 + 3,490

ADMISSION INFO (1991/92 PRICES)
Adult Standing: £6 Members   £6.50 Non-members
Adult Seating: £8 Members   £9 or £10 Non-members
Child Standing: £4 Members   £6.50 Non-members
Child Seating: £4.00 in Family Stands
Programme Price: £1.20
FAX Number: (0702) 330164

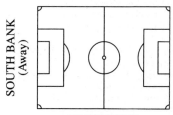

SHAKESPEARE DRIVE
WEST STAND

SOUTH BANK
(Away)

FAIRFAX DRIVE
NORTH BANK

EAST STAND
VICTORIA AVENUE

Travelling Supporters Information:
Routes: From North & West: Take A127 into Southend then at roundabout take 3rd exit into Victoria
Avenue; From South: Take A13 following signs for Southend and turn left into West Road. At the end of
West Road turn left into Victoria Avenue.

STOCKPORT COUNTY FC

Founded: 1883
Turned Professional: 1891
Limited Company: 1908
Admitted to League: 1900
Former Name(s): Heaton Norris Rovers FC;
Heaton Norris FC
Nickname: 'Hatters' 'County'
Ground: Edgeley Park, Hardcastle Road,
Edgeley, Stockport   SK3 9DD

Record Attendance: 27,833 (11/2/50)
Colours: Shirts - Blue with Red & Blue Flashes
Shorts - White
Telephone No.: (061) 480-8888
Ticket Information: (061) 480-8888
Pitch Size: 111 × 71yds
Ground Capacity: 8,500
Seating Capacity: 1,800

GENERAL INFORMATION
Supporters Club Administrator:
Simon Dawson
Address: c/o Club Shop
Telephone Number: (061) 480-8117
Car Parking: Street Parking
Coach Parking: By Police Direction
Nearest Railway Station: Stockport
(5 minutes walk)
Nearest Bus Station: Mersey Square
(10 minutes walk)
Club Shop: (061) 480-8117
Opening Times: Weekdays 9.00-5.00pm
Saturdays 9.30-12.30pm
Telephone No.: (061) 480-8117
Postal Sales: Yes
Nearest Police Station: Stockport (1 mile)
Police Force: Greater Manchester
Police Telephone No.: (061) 872-5050

GROUND INFORMATION
Away Supporters' Entrances: Railway End
Turnstiles
Away Supporters' Sections: Railway End
Family Facilities: **Location of Stand**:
In front of Main Stand
Capacity of Stand: 1,800

ADMISSION INFO (1992/93 PRICES)
Adult Standing: £6.00
Adult Seating: £9.00
Child Standing: £4.00
Child Seating: £5.00
Programme Price: £1.00
FAX Number: (061) 480-0230

POPULAR SIDE

RAILWAY END
(Away)

CHEADLE END

MAIN STAND
HARDCASTLE ROAD

Travelling Supporters Information:
Routes: From North, South & West: Exit M63 junction 11 and join A560, following signs for Cheadle, after 0.25 mile turn right into Edgeley Road and in 1 mile turn right into Caroline Street for Ground; From
East: Take A6 or A560 into Stockport Town Centre and turn left into Greek Street. Take 2nd exit into Mer-
cian Way (from roundabout) then turn left into Caroline Street - Ground straight ahead.

STOKE CITY FC

Founded: 1863
Turned Professional: 1885
Limited Company: 1908
Admitted to League: 1888 (Founder)
Former Name(s): Stoke FC
Nickname: 'Potters'
Ground: Victoria Ground, Boothen Old Road, Stoke-on-Trent ST4 4EG

Record Attendance: 51,380 (29/3/37)
Colours: Shirts - Red & White Stripes
Shorts - White
Telephone No.: (0782) 413511
Ticket Information: (0782) 413961
Pitch Size: 116 × 72yds
Ground Capacity: 25,084
Seating Capacity: 9,625

GENERAL INFORMATION

Supporters Club Administrator:
Nic Mansfield
Address: 11A Westland Street, Penkhull,
Stoke-on-Trent ST4 7HE
Telephone Number: (0782) 744674
Car Parking: Car Park at Ground (2,000 cars)
Coach Parking: Whieldon Road
Nearest Railway Station: Stoke-on-Trent
(10 minutes walk)
Nearest Bus Station: Hanley (2 miles)
Club Shop:
Opening Times: Monday to Friday 9.30-5.00
Saturdays 9.30-12.00
Telephone No.: (0782) 747078
Postal Sales: Yes
Nearest Police Station: Stoke-on-Trent
(0.25 mile)
Police Force: Staffordshire
Police Telephone No.: (0782) 744644

GROUND INFORMATION

Away Supporters' Entrances: Butler Street
Turnstiles
Away Supporters' Sections: Butler Street Stand &
Stoke End Paddock
Family Facilities: **Location of Stand**:
Stoke End Stand
Capacity of Stand: 2,000

ADMISSION INFO (1992/93 PRICES)

Adult Standing: £6.00
Adult Seating: £9.00
Child Standing: £4.50
Child Seating: £6.00
Programme Price: £1.00
FAX Number: (0782) 46422

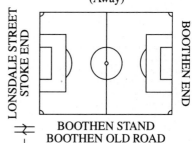

Travelling Supporters Information:
Routes: From North, South & West: Exit M6 junction 15 and follow signs Stoke (A5006) and join A500. Branch left 0.75 mile and take 2nd exit at roundabout into Campbell Road for Ground; From East: Take A50 into Stoke Town Centre and turn left at crossroads into Lonsdale Street for Campbell Road.

SUNDERLAND AFC

Founded: 1879
Turned Professional: 1886
Limited Company: 1906
Admitted to League: 1890
Former Name(s): Sunderland & District Teachers FC
Nickname: 'Rokerites'
Ground: Roker Park, Grantham Road, Roker Sunderland   SR6 9SW

Record Attendance: 75,118 (8/3/33)
Colours: Shirts - Red & White Stripes
Shorts - Black
Telephone No.: (091) 514-0332
Ticket Information: (091) 514-0332
Pitch Size: 113 × 74yds
Ground Capacity: 31,222
Seating Capacity: 7,753

GENERAL INFORMATION
Supporters Club Administrator:
Audrey Baillie
Address: 36 Roker Baths Road, Roker, Sunderland
Telephone Number: (091) 567-0067
Car Parking: Car Park for 1,500 cars
Coach Parking: Seafront, Roker
Nearest Railway Station: Seaburn
Nearest Bus Station: Town Centre (2 miles)
Club Shop: Town Centre & Roker Park
Opening Times: Monday-Saturday 9.00-5.00
Telephone No.: (091) 567-2336
Postal Sales: Yes
Nearest Police Station: Southwick (1.25 ml)
Police Force: Northumbria
Police Telephone No.: (091) 567-6155

GROUND INFORMATION
Away Supporters' Entrances: Roker End Turnstiles
Away Supporters' Sections: Roker End
Family Facilities: Location of Stand:
Centre Stand
Capacity of Stand: 1,200

ADMISSION INFO (1991/92 PRICES)
Adult Standing: £6.00 Members   £7 Non-members
Adult Seating: £10.00
Child Standing: £3.00
Child Seating: £10.00   (Family Enclosure £6.00)
Programme Price: £1.00
FAX Number: (091) 514-5854

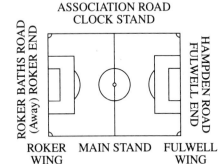

Travelling Supporters Information:
Routes: From North: Take A184 - Sunderland. Through Boldon 0.25 mile after Greyhound Stadium at roundabout, straight on for Town Centre (A1018). Left at 'T' junction. At traffic lights (Blue Bell Pub) turn right. Follow road for 0.75 mile and turn left, sign posted for Roker Park; From South: A19 or A1M take turn-off for A1231 Sunderland North. A1M-A690 Sunderland, left into A19 towards Tyne Tunnel & Gateshead. Take A1231 Sunderland North, then follow signs for Town Centre. After 2 miles at traffic lights, straight ahead in left lane marked A1289 Roker. After 1 mile follow Roker A183 signs. After 200 yards follow signs for Whitburn & Sea Front (A183). After 0.5 mile turn left down side street, the Football Ground is straight ahead.

SWANSEA CITY FC

Founded: 1900	**Record Attendance**: 32,796 (17/2/68)
Turned Professional: 1912	**Colours**: Shirts - White
Limited Company: 1912	Shorts - White
Admitted to League: 1920	**Telephone No.**: (0792) 474114
Former Name(s): Swansea Town FC	**Ticket Information**: (0792) 474114
(1900-1970)	**Pitch Size**: 110 × 74yds
Nickname: 'Swans'	**Ground Capacity**: 16,419
Ground: Vetch Field, Swansea SA1 3SU	**Seating Capacity**: 3,414

GENERAL INFORMATION
Supporters Club Administrator:
John Button
Address: 159 Western Street, Swansea
Telephone Number: (0792) 460958
Car Parking: Kingsway Car Park (200 yards)
Coach Parking: By Police Direction
Nearest Railway Station: Swansea High
Street (0.5 mile)
Nearest Bus Station: Quadrant Depot
(0.25 mile)
Club Shop: 33 William
Street, Swansea SA1 3QS
Opening Times: Weekdays 9.30-4.30
Matchdays 9.30-5.00
Telephone No.: (0792) 462584
Postal Sales: Yes
Nearest Police Station: Swansea Central
(0.5 mile)
Police Force: South Wales
Police Telephone No.: (0792) 456999

GROUND INFORMATION
Away Supporters' Entrances: Richardson Street
Turnstiles
Away Supporters' Sections: West Terrace Enclosure
- Partially covered
Family Facilities: Location of Stand:
Jewson Family Enclosure (West Side of Centre Stand)
Capacity of Stand: 321 seats

ADMISSION INFO (1992/93 PRICES)
Adult Standing: £5.00
Adult Seating: £7.50 - £8.00
Child Standing: £2.50
Child Seating: Family + 1 = £11.00   + 2 = £12.50
Programme Price: £1.00
FAX Number: (0792) 646120

MADOC STREET
NORTH BANK

RICHARDSON STREET
WEST TERRACE
(Away)

WILLIAM STREET
EAST STAND

CENTRE STAND
GLAMORGAN STREET

Travelling Supporters Information:
Routes: From All Parts: Exit M4 junction 45 and follow Swansea (A4067) signs into City Centre along
High Street. Passing Railway Station into Castle Station then Wind Street and take 3rd exit at roundabout into
Victoria Road and bear right towards bus station at Quadrant for Ground.

SWINDON TOWN FC

Founded: 1881	**Record Attendance**: 32,000 (15/1/72)
Turned Professional: 1895	**Colours**: Shirts - Red
Limited Company: 1897	Shorts - Red
Admitted to League: 1920	**Telephone No.**: (0793) 430430
Former Name(s): None	**Ticket Information**: (0793) 430430
Nickname: 'Robins'	**Pitch Size**: 114 × 72yds
Ground: County Ground, County Road,	**Ground Capacity**: 16,432
Swindon SN1 2ED	**Seating Capacity**: 7,500

GENERAL INFORMATION
Supporters Club Administrator:
Miss S. Cobern
Address: 31 Pewsham Road, Penhill,
Swindon
Telephone Number: (0793) 481061
Car Parking: Car Park Adjacent
Coach Parking: Car Park Adjacent
Nearest Railway Station: Swindon (0.5 mile)
Nearest Bus Station: Swindon (0.5 mile)
Club Shop: Robins Corner
Opening Times: Weekdays 10.00 - 4.00pm
Saturdays 9.00-3.00pm on matchdays only
Telephone No.: (0793) 430430
Postal Sales: Yes
Nearest Police Station: Fleming Way,
Swindon
Police Force: Wiltshire
Police Telephone No.: (0793) 528111

GROUND INFORMATION
Away Supporters' Entrances: Visitors Enclosure
Turnstiles - Stratton Bank
Away Supporters' Sections: Visitors Enclosure
Stratton Bank (Part open)
Family Facilities: **Location of Stand**:
Town End Stand
Capacity of Stand: 500

ADMISSION INFO (1992/93 PRICES)
Adult Standing: £6 Members   £7.50 Non members
Adult Seating: Members Only £7.50 - £10.50
Child Standing: £4 Members   £7.50 Non-members
Child Seating: Members Only £5.00 - £10.50
Programme Price: £1.00
FAX Number: (0793) 536170

```
            NORTH STAND
     ┌──────────────────────┐
 C T │  ┌─┐            ┌─┐  │ S H  S  A
 O O │  │ │      o     │ │  │ T o  T  w
 U W │  │ │     (o)    │ │  │ R m  R  a
 N N │  └─┘            └─┘  │ A e  A  y
 T   │                      │ T )  T
 Y E │                      │ T    T
 R N │                      │ O    O
 O D │  ┌─┐            ┌─┐  │ N    N
 A   │  │ │      o     │ │  │      B
 D   │  └─┘            └─┘  │      A
     └──────────────────────┘      N K
            SOUTH STAND
          SHRIVENHAM ROAD
```

Travelling Supporters Information:
Routes: From London & East & South: Exit M4 junction 15 and take A345 into Swindon along Queen's Drive, take 3rd exit at 'Magic Roundabout' into County Road; From West: Exit M4 junction 15 then as above; From North: Take M4 or A345/A420/A361 to County Road roundabout then as above.

TORQUAY UNITED FC

Founded: 1898	**Record Attendance**: 21,908 (29/1/55)
Turned Professional: 1921	**Colours**: Shirts - Yellow & White Stripe
Limited Company: 1921	Shorts - Navy
Admitted to League: 1927	**Telephone No.**: (0803) 328666/7
Former Name(s): Torquay Town (1898-1910)	**Ticket Information**: (0803) 328666/7
Nickname: 'Gulls'	**Pitch Size**: 112 × 74yds
Ground: Plainmoor Ground, Torquay	**Ground Capacity**: 6,000
TQ1 3PS	**Seating Capacity**: 1,476

GENERAL INFORMATION

Supporters Club Chairman: Mr. S. Drylie
Address: 7 Bove Park Road, Torquay
Telephone Number: (0803) 316294
Car Parking: Street Parking
Coach Parking: Lymington Road Coach
Station (0.5 mile)
Nearest Railway Station: Torquay (2 miles)
Nearest Bus Station: Lymington Road
(0.5 mile)
Club Shop:
Opening Times: Matchdays & During Office
Hours
Telephone No.: (0803) 328666
Postal Sales: Yes
Nearest Police Station: Torquay (1 mile)
Police Force: Devon & Cornwall
Police Telephone No.: (0803) 214491

GROUND INFORMATION

Away Supporters' Entrances: Babbacombe End
Turnstiles
Away Supporters' Sections: Babbacombe End
Family Facilities: **Location of Stand**:
Ellacombe End - Torcroft Family Stand
Capacity of Stand: 500 (Family Part)

ADMISSION INFO (1991/92 PRICES)

Adult Standing: £6.00
Adult Seating: £6.00
Child Standing: £3.00
Child Seating: £3.00
Programme Price: £1.00
FAX Number: (0803) 323976

Travelling Supporters Information:

Routes: From North & East: Take M5 to A38 and A380 to Kingskerwell. Take 1st exit at roundabout (1 mile) and in 1 mile turn left following Babbacombe (A3022) signs. Turn left (0.75 mile) into Westhill Road for Warbro Road; From West: Take A380 into Town Centre and follow signs Teignmouth (A379) to Lymington Road. Turn right into Upton Hill and follow into Bronshill Road. Take 2nd left into Derwent Road and at end turn right and right again into Marnham Road.

TOTTENHAM HOTSPUR FC

Founded: 1882
Turned Professional: 1895
Limited Company: 1898
Admitted to League: 1908
Former Name(s): Hotspur FC (1882-85)
Nickname: 'Spurs'
Ground: White Hart Lane, 748 High Road, Tottenham, London N17 0AP

Record Attendance: 75,038 (5/3/38)
Colours: Shirts - White
　　　　　Shorts - Navy Blue
Telephone No.: (081) 808-6666
Ticket Office: (081) 808-8080
Pitch Size: 110 × 73yds
Ground Capacity: 30,000 Approximately
Seating Capacity: 30,000 Approximately

GENERAL INFORMATION

Supporters Club Administrator:
Sue Sharples and Linda Watkins
Address: Spurs Members Club, 7526 High Road, Tottenham N17
Telephone Number: (081) 808-8080
Car Parking: None within 0.25 mile
Coach Parking: Northumberland Park Coach Park
Nearest Railway Station: White Hart Lane (Nearby)
Nearest Tube Station: Seven Sisters (Victoria); Manor House (Piccadilly)
Club Shop:
Opening Times: Weekdays 9.30-5.30 and Matchdays 9.30-6.00
Telephone No.: (081) 801-1669
Postal Sales: Yes
Nearest Police Station: Tottenham (1 mile)
Police Force: Metropolitan
Police Telephone No.: (081) 801-3443

GROUND INFORMATION

Away Supporters' Entrances: Park Lane, Turnstiles 60-65 (seating only)
Away Supporters' Sections: South Stand, Park Lane
Family Facilities:　**Location of Stand**:
Members Stand
Capacity of Stand: 4,407 Standing; 4,357 Seats

ADMISSION INFO (1992/93 PRICES)

Adult Standing: Members Only £8.00
Adult Seating: £12.00 - £19.00 (Members £11.00)
Child Standing: Members Only £4.00
Child Seating: Members Only £5.00
Programme Price: £1.50
FAX Number: (081) 885-1951

Travelling Supporters Information:
Routes:　From All Parts:　Take A406 North Circular to Edmonton and at traffic lights follow signs for Tottenham (A1010) into Fore Street for Ground.

TRANMERE ROVERS FC

Founded: 1881
Turned Professional: 1912
Limited Company: 1920
Admitted to League: 1921
Former Name(s): Belmont FC
Nickname: 'Rovers'
Ground: Prenton Park, Prenton Road West, Birkenhead   L42 9PN

Record Attendance: 24,424 (5/2/72)
Colours: Shirts - White
　　　　　　Shorts - White
Telephone No.: (051) 608-3677
Ticket Information: (051) 608-3677
Pitch Size: 112 × 74yds
Ground Capacity: 14,200
Seating Capacity: 3,800

GENERAL INFORMATION
Supporters Club Administrator: A. Price
Address: c/o Club
Telephone Number: (051) 608-3677
Car Parking: Large Car Park at Ground
Coach Parking: At Ground
Nearest Railway Station: Hamilton Square, Rock Ferry (1 mile)
Nearest Bus Station: Birkenhead
Club Shop:
Opening Times: Weekdays & Matchdays 9.00-5.00
Telephone No.: (051) 608-0438
Postal Sales: Yes
Nearest Police Station: Bebington (2 miles)
Police Force: Merseyside
Police Telephone No.: (051) 709-6010

GROUND INFORMATION
Away Supporters' Entrances: Bebington End Turnstiles - access from Main Car Park
Away Supporters' Sections: Bebington End (open)
Family Facilities: Location of Stand:
Family Enclosure
Capacity of Stand: 3,800

ADMISSION INFO (1992/93 PRICES)
Adult Standing: £6.00
Adult Seating: £8.00
Child Standing: £5.00
Child Seating: £6.00
Programme Price: £1.00
FAX Number: (051) 608-4385

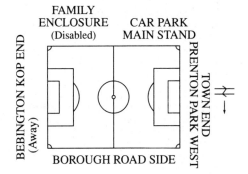

Travelling Supporters Information:
Routes: From North: Take Mersey Tunnel to M53, exit junction 3 and take 1st exit at roundabout (A552), in 1.25 mile turn right at crossroads (B5151) then left into Prenton Road West; From South & East: Exit M53 junction 4 and take 4th exit at roundabout (B5151). After 2.5 miles turn right into Prenton Road West.

WALSALL FC

Founded: 1888	**Record Attendance**: 10,628 (20/5/91)
Turned Professional: 1888	(England B vs. Switzerland)
Limited Company: 1921	**Colours**: Shirts - Red
Admitted to League: 1892	Shorts - White
Former Name(s): Walsall Town Swifts FC	**Telephone No.**: (0922) 22791
(1888-95)	**Ticket Information**: (0922) 22791
Nickname: 'Saddlers'	**Pitch Size**: 110 × 73yds
Ground: Bescot Stadium, Bescot Crescent,	**Ground Capacity**: 10,400
Walsall, West Midlands WS1 4SA	**Seating Capacity**: 4,500

GENERAL INFORMATION
Supporters Club Administrator:
John Wilson
Address: Saddlers Club, Wallows Lane,
Walsall
Telephone Number: (0922) 22257
Car Parking: Car Park at Ground
Coach Parking: At Ground
Nearest Railway Station: Bescot (Adjacent)
Nearest Bus Station: Bradford Place, Walsall
Club Shop:
Opening Times: Weekdays 10.00-2.00pm
and Matchdays 9.30-5.15pm
Telephone No.: (0922) 22791
Postal Sales: Yes
Nearest Police Station: Walsall (2 miles)
Police Force: West Midlands
Police Telephone No.: (0922) 38111

GROUND INFORMATION
Away Supporters' Entrances: William Sharp Stand
Turnstiles 21-28
Away Supporters' Sections: Highgate Mild Stand 1-2
(Seating); William Sharp Stand (Standing)
Family Facilities: **Location of Stand**:
In front of Highgate Mild Stand - Blocks A & B
Capacity of Stand: 448 Seats

ADMISSION INFO (1992/93 PRICES)
Adult Standing: £6.00
Adult Seating: £7.50 - £8.50
Child Standing: £5.00
Child Seating: £5.00 - £8.50
Programme Price: £1.00
FAX Number: (0922) 613202

HIGHGATE MILD STAND
(Away)

GILBERT ALSO STAND

(BESCOT CRESCENT)
WILLIAM SHARP STAND
(Away)

H.L. FELLOWS STAND

Travelling Supporters Information:
Routes: From All Parts: Exit M6 junction 9 turning North towards Walsall onto the A461. After 0.25 mile turn right into Wallows Lane and pass over Railway Bridge. Then take 1st right into Bescot Crescent and ground is 0.5 mile along on left adjacent to Bescot Railway Station.

WATFORD FC

Founded: 1891
Turned Professional: 1897
Limited Company: 1909
Admitted to League: 1920
Former Name(s): Formed by Amalgamation of
West Herts FC & St Mary's FC
Nickname: 'Hornets'
Ground: Vicarage Road Stadium, Watford
WD1 8ER

Record Attendance: 34,099 (3/2/69)
Colours: Shirts - Yellow with Black & Red
Shorts - Red with Yellow & Black
Telephone No.: (0923) 230933
Ticket Information: (0923) 220393
Pitch Size: 115 × 75yds
Ground Capacity: 23,596
Seating Capacity: 6,906

GENERAL INFORMATION
Supporters Club Administrator:
Allan Robson
Address: c/o Club
Telephone Number: (0923) 230933
Car Parking: Nearby Multi-Storey Car Park
Coach Parking: Cardiff Road Car Park
Nearest Railway Station: Station at Ground
(for Big Games only)
Nearest Bus Station: Watford
Club Shop:
Opening Times: Tuesday to Saturday
9.00-5.00
Telephone No.: (0923) 220847
Postal Sales: Yes
Nearest Police Station: Shady Lane,
Clarendon Road, Watford (1.5 miles)
Police Force: Hertfordshire
Police Telephone No.: (0923) 244444

GROUND INFORMATION
Away Supporters' Entrances: Entrance Z
Away Supporters' Sections: South West Terrace
(Partially covered)
Family Facilities: Location of Stand:
East Stand
Capacity of Stand: 750 Seated in Family Block,
1,250 in Family Terrace

ADMISSION INFO (1992/93 PRICES)
Adult Standing: £6.00 or £7.00
Adult Seating: £8.00 - £10.00
Child Standing: £3.00 (Family Terrace) - £7.00
Child Seating: £5.00 (Family Enclosure) - £10.00
Programme Price: £1.30
FAX Number: (0923) 239759

ROUS STAND

SOUTH TERRACE (Away)

VICARAGE ROAD

(FAMILY ENCLOSURE)
OCCUPATION ROAD
EAST STAND

Travelling Supporters Information:
Routes: From North: Exit M1 junction 6 following signs for Watford A405/A41 & A411. Follow signs
Slough A412 and turn left (0.75 mile) into Harwoods Road. Turn left at 'T' junction into Vicarage Road;
From South & East: Exit M1 junction 5 and follow signs for Watford (A41) & A412. Follow signs for
Slough (then as North); From West: Take A412 past Croxley Green Station and turn right (1 mile) into Har-
woods Road (then as North).

WEST BROMWICH ALBION FC

Founded: 1879
Turned Professional: 1885
Limited Company: 1892
Admitted to League: 1888 (Founder)
Former Name(s): West Bromwich Strollers (1879-1880)
Nickname: 'Throstles' 'Baggies' 'Albion'
Ground: The Hawthorns, Halfords Lane, West Bromwich, West Midlands   B71 4LF

Record Attendance: 64,815 (6/3/37)
Colours: Shirts - Navy Blue & White Stripes
Shorts - White
Telephone No.: (021) 525-8888
Ticket Information: (021) 553-5472
Pitch Size: 115 × 75yds
Ground Capacity: 33,781
Seating Capacity: 10,397

GENERAL INFORMATION
Supporters Club Administrator:
David Knott
Address: c/o 44 Hollyhedge Road, West Bromwich, West Midlands   B71 3AB
Telephone Number: (0384) 292333
Car Parking: Halfords Lane Car Parks, Rainbow Stand Car Park
Coach Parking: Rainbow Stand Car Park
Nearest Railway Station: Rolfe Street, Smethwick (1.5 miles)
Nearest Bus Station: Town Centre
Club Shop:
Opening Times: Weekdays 9.00-5.00
Matchdays 9.00-2.45
Telephone No.: (021) 525-2145
Postal Sales: Yes
Nearest Police Station: Holyhead Road, Handsworth (0.5 mile)
Police Force: West Midlands
Police Telephone No.: (021) 554-3414

GROUND INFORMATION
Away Supporters' Entrances: Smethwick End Turnstiles (P-block) & Entrance Q - Rainbow Stand
Away Supporters' Sections: Smethwick End Terrace (Covered standing) & Rainbow Stand (seating)
Family Facilities: **Location of Stand**: Halfords Lane Stand (M Block) (Home support. only)
Capacity of Stand: 432

ADMISSION INFO (1992/93 PRICES)
Adult Standing: £6.50
Adult Seating: £7.50 - £9.00
Child Standing: £3.50
Child Seating: £4.50 - £5.00
Programme Price: £1.00
FAX Number: (021) 553-6634
Note : Members' prices 50p less than those shown.

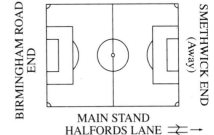

Travelling Supporters Information:
Routes: From All Parts: Exit M5 junction 1 and take Birmingham Road (A41) for Ground.

WEST HAM UNITED FC

Founded: 1895	**Record Attendance**: 42,322 (17/10/70)
Turned Professional: 1900	**Colours**: Shirts - Claret & Blue
Limited Company: 1900	Shorts - White
Admitted to League: 1919	**Telephone No.**: (081) 472-2740
Former Name(s): Thames Iron Works F.C.	**Ticket Information**: (081) 472-3322
Nickname: 'Hammers'	**Pitch Size**: 112 × 72yds
Ground: Boleyn Ground, Green Street,	**Ground Capacity**: 22,503
Upton Park, London E13 9AZ	**Seating Capacity**: 11,600

GENERAL INFORMATION

Supporters Club Administrator:
Mr. T. Jenkinson
Address: West Ham Supporters' Club,
Castle Street, East Ham   E6
Telephone Number: (081) 472-1680
Car Parking: Street Parking
Coach Parking: By Police Direction
Nearest Railway Station: Barking
Nearest Tube Station: Upton Park (5 mins.)
Club Shop: The Hammers Shop
Opening Times: Weekdays & Matchdays
9.30-5.30
Telephone No.: (081) 472-4214
Postal Sales: Yes
Nearest Police Station: East Ham High Street
South (0.5 mile)
Police Force: Metropolitan
Police Telephone No.: (081) 593-8232

GROUND INFORMATION

Away Supporters' Entrances: Turnstiles 23-29,
Castle Street
Away Supporters' Sections: South Bank West Side
(Partially covered)
Family Facilities: **Location of Stand**:
East Stand Side
Capacity of Stand: 905

ADMISSION INFO (1992/93 PRICES)

Adult Standing: £9.00
Adult Seating: £12.00, £14.00, £16.00 or £18.00
Child Standing: £5.00 (Junior Hammer Members)
Child Seating: Same as adults
Programme Price: £1.50
FAX Number: (081) 471-2997

Travelling Supporters Information:
Routes: From North & West: Take North Circular (A406) to A124 (East Ham) then along Barking Road for approximately 1.5 miles until approaching traffic lights at crossroad. Turn right into Green Street, ground is on right-hand side; From South: Take Blackwall Tunnel and A13 to Canning Town. Follow signs for East Ham (A124). After 1.75 miles turn left into Green Street; From East: Take A13 and turn right onto A117 at crossroads. After approximately 1 mile turn left at crossroads onto A124. Turn right (0.75 mile) into Green Street.

WIGAN ATHLETIC AFC

Founded: 1932	**Record Attendance**: 27,500 (12/12/51)
Turned Professional: 1932	**Colours**: Shirts - Blue
Limited Company: 1986	Shorts - Blue with White/Red Trim
Admitted to League: 1978	**Telephone No.**: (0942) 44433
Former Name(s): None	**Ticket Information**: (0942) 44433
Nickname: 'Latics'	**Pitch Size**: 117 × 73yds
Ground: Springfield Park, Wigan, Lancs.	**Ground Capacity**: 12,500
WN6 7BA	**Seating Capacity**: 1,272

GENERAL INFORMATION
Supporters Club Administrator: Joe Mills
Address: c/o Club
Telephone Number: (0942) 43512
Car Parking: Street Parking
Coach Parking: Shevington End
Nearest Railway Station: Wallgate & North West (1 mile)
Nearest Bus Station: Wigan
Club Shop:
Opening Times: Weekdays & Matchdays 9.00-5.00
Telephone No.: (0942) 44433
Postal Sales: Yes
Nearest Police Station: Harrogate Street, Wigan (1 mile)
Police Force: Greater Manchester
Police Telephone No.: (0942) 44981

GROUND INFORMATION
Away Supporters' Entrances: Shevington End Turnstiles
Away Supporters' Sections: Shevington End (Partially covered)
Family Facilities: **Location of Stand**: In front of Phoenix Stand (Heinz Family Enclosure)
Capacity of Stand: 128

ADMISSION INFO (1992/93 PRICES)
Adult Standing: £5.50
Adult Seating: £7.00
Child Standing: £3.00
Child Seating: £5.00
Programme Price: £1.00
FAX Number: (0942) 494654

```
        HEINZ
        FAMILY
      ENCLOSURE
      (Disabled)       PHOENIX STAND

 SHEVINGTON ROAD   ┌──────────────────┐   SHEVINGTON ROAD
       TOWN END    │   │          │   │      (Away)
                   │   │    ( )   │   │
                   └──────────────────┘
        SHEVINGTON ROAD
                    POPULAR SIDE
                  ST. ANDREWS DRIVE
```

Travelling Supporters Information:
Routes: From North: Exit M6 junction 27 following signs for Wigan (A5209), turn right (0.25 mile) (B5206). Turn left 1 mile and in 4.5 miles take left into Springfield Road; From South: Exit M6 junction 25 following signs for Wigan (A49). Turn left into Robin Park Road and into Scot Lane. Turn right at 3rd traffic lights into Woodhouse Lane and left at traffic lights into Springfield Road; From East: Take A557 into Town Centre then left into Robin Park Road (then as South).

WIMBLEDON FC

Founded: 1889	**Record Attendance**: 18,000 (1934-35)
Turned Professional: 1964	**Colours**: Shirts - Blue
Limited Company: 1964	Shorts - Blue
Admitted to League: 1977	**Telephone No.**: (081) 771-2233
Former Name(s): Wimbledon Old Centrals	**Ticket Information**: (081) 771-8841
FC (1889-1905)	**Pitch Size**: 110 × 75yds
Nickname: 'Dons'	**Ground Capacity**: 29,949
Ground: Selhurst Park, London SE25 6PU	**Seating Capacity**: 15,135

GENERAL INFORMATION
Supporters Club Administrator:
Sue Moody
Address: c/o Club
Telephone Number: (081) 771-2233
Car Parking: Street Parking
Coach Parking: Thornton Heath
Nearest Railway Station: Selhurst/Norwood
Junction/Thornton Heath
Club Shop:
Opening Times: Weekdays & Matchdays
9.30-5.30
Telephone No.: (081) 653-5584
Postal Sales: Yes
Nearest Police Station: South Norwood
(15 minutes walk)
Police Force: Metropolitan
Police Telephone No.: (081) 653-8568

GROUND INFORMATION
Away Supporters' Entrances: Park Road/Homesdale
Road
Away Supporters' Sections: Corner - Park Road &
Holmesdale Road (Open Terrace & Covered Seating)
Family Facilities: **Location of Stand**:
Members Stand (Clifton Road End)
Capacity of Stand: 4,600

ADMISSION INFO (1992/93 PRICES)
Adult Standing: £7.00 or £8.00
Adult Seating: £15.00 - £20.00
Child Standing: £4.00 or £5.00
Child Seating: £8.00 - £10.00
Programme Price: £1.00
FAX Number: (081) 768-0641

Travelling Supporters Information:
Routes: From North: Take M1/A1 to North Circular (A406) to Chiswick. Take South Circular (A205) to
Wandsworth, take A3 to A214 and follow signs to Streatham to A23. Turn left onto B273 (1 mile), follow to
end and turn left into High Street and into Whitehorse Lane; From East: Take A232 (Croydon Road) to
Shirley and join A215 (Norwood Road), after 2.25 miles take left into Whitehorse Lane; From South: Take
A23 and follow signs Crystal Palace B266 through Thornton Heath into Whitehorse Lane; From West: Take
M4 to Chiswick (then as North).

WOLVERHAMPTON WANDERERS FC

Founded: 1877	**Record Attendance**: 61,315 (11/2/39)
Turned Professional: 1888	**Colours**: Shirts - Gold
Limited Company: 1892	Shorts - Black
Admitted to League: 1888 (Founder)	**Telephone No.**: (0902) 712181
Former Name(s): St. Luke's FC & The	**Ticket Information**: (0902) 25899
Wanderers FC (combined 1880)	**Pitch Size**: 116 × 74yds
Nickname: 'Wolves'	**Ground Capacity**: 25,000
Ground: Molineux Ground, Waterloo Road,	**Seating Capacity**: 14,600
Wolverhampton WV1 4QR	

GENERAL INFORMATION
Supporters Club Administrator: Albert Bates
Address: 341 Penn Road, Penn, Wolverhampton
Telephone Number: (0902) 330322
Car Parking: Around West Park & Rear of North Bank
Coach Parking: By Police Direction
Nearest Railway Station: Wolverhampton (1 mile)
Nearest Bus Station: Wolverhampton (0.25 mile)
Club Shop:
Opening Times: Weekdays & Matchdays 9.00-5.00
Telephone No.: (0902) 27524
Postal Sales: Yes
Nearest Police Station: Dunstall Road, (500 yards)
Police Force: West Midlands
Police Telephone No.: (0902) 27851

GROUND INFORMATION
Away Supporters' Entrances: South Bank Turnstiles
Away Supporters' Sections: South Bank (Partially Covered)
Family Facilities: **Location of Stand**: John Ireland Lower Tier
Capacity of Stand: 3,000

ADMISSION INFO (1992/93 PRICES)
Adult Standing: £6.00
Adult Seating: £6.00 - £8.00
Child Standing: £4.00
Child Seating: £5.00 (Family Enclosure) - £8.00
Programme Price: £1.00
FAX Number: (0902) 24612

Travelling Supporters Information:
Routes: From North: Exit M6 junction 12 following signs for Wolverhampton A5, then A449 and at roundabout take 2nd exit into Waterloo Road then turn left into Molineux Street; From South: Exit M5 junction 2 following signs for Wolverhampton A4123, turn right, then left into Ring Road, turn left (1 mile) into Waterloo Road, then turn right into Molineux Street; from East: Exit M6 junction 10 following signs Wolverhampton A454, turn right at crossroads into Stratford Street then turn left (0.25 mile) into Ring Road, right at crossroads into Waterloo Road then right into Molineux Street; From West: Take A454 and at roundabout turn left into Ring Road (then as East).

WREXHAM FC

Founded: 1873
Turned Professional: 1912
Limited Company: 1912
Admitted to League: 1921
Former Name(s): None
Nickname: 'Robins'
Ground: Racecourse Ground, Mold Road, Wrexham, Clwyd

Record Attendance: 34,445 (26/1/57)
Colours: Shirts - Red
　　　　　 Shorts - White
Telephone No.: (0978) 262129
Ticket Information: (0978) 262129
Pitch Size: 111 × 71yds
Ground Capacity: 17,500
Seating Capacity: 5,026

GENERAL INFORMATION

Supporters Club Administrator: Miss Ena Williams
Address: c/o Club
Telephone Number: (0978) 263111
Car Parking: Town Car Parks Nearby
Coach Parking: -
Nearest Railway Station: Wrexham General (Adjacent)
Nearest Bus Station: Wrexham
Club Shop: Promotions Office
Opening Times: Matchdays Only
Telephone No.: (0978) 352536
Postal Sales: Yes
Nearest Police Station: Bodhyfryd (HQ) (1 mile)
Police Force: Wrexham Division
Police Telephone No.: (0978) 290222

GROUND INFORMATION

Away Supporters' Entrances: Mold End Turnstiles
Away Supporters' Sections: Marstons Stand, Mold End (Covered)
Family Facilities: Location of Stand: Yale Stand Town End
Capacity of Stand: 280

ADMISSION INFO (1992/93 PRICES)

Adult Standing: £5.00
Adult Seating: £7.00
Child Standing: £3.50
Child Seating: £5.00
Programme Price: £1.00
FAX Number: (0978) 357821
Note : Ground redevelopment may be undertaken during the 1992/93 season.

Travelling Supporters Information:
Routes: From North & West: Take A483 and Wrexham Bypass to junction with A541. Branch left and at roundabout follow Wrexham signs into Mold Road; From South & East: Take A525 or A534 into Wrexham then follow A541 signs into Mold Road.

YORK CITY FC

Founded: 1922	**Record Attendance**: 28,123 (5/3/38)
Turned Professional: 1922	**Colours**: Shirts - Red
Limited Company: 1922	Shorts - Blue
Admitted to League: 1929	**Telephone No.**: (0904) 624447
Former Name(s): None	**Ticket Information**: (0904) 624447
Nickname: 'Minstermen'	**Pitch Size**: 115 × 75yds
Ground: Bootham Crescent, York YO3 7AQ	**Ground Capacity**: 12,760
	Seating Capacity: 3,059

GENERAL INFORMATION

Supporters Club Administrator: Raymond Wynn
Address: 155 Manor Drive North, York
Telephone Number: (0904) 797578
Car Parking: Street Parking
Coach Parking: By Police Direction
Nearest Railway Station: York (1 mile)
Nearest Bus Station: York
Club Shop:
Opening Times: Monday to Wednesday 9.00-5.00; Thursday to Friday 9.00-1.00; Saturday Matchdays 1.00-3.00 + 4.40-5.30
Telephone No.: (0904) 645941
Postal Sales: Yes
Nearest Police Station: Fulford
Police Force: North Yorkshire
Police Telephone No.: (0904) 631321

GROUND INFORMATION

Away Supporters' Entrances: Grosvenor Road Turnstiles
Away Supporters' Sections: Grosvenor Road End, Bootham Crescent
Family Facilities: **Location of Stand**: None
Capacity of Stand: -

ADMISSION INFO (1992/93 PRICES)

Adult Standing: £5.00 or £5.50
Adult Seating: £6.00 or £8.00
Child Standing: £3.00 or £3.50 (Members Only)
Child Seating: £4.00 or £5.00 (Members Only)
Programme Price: £1.00
FAX Number: (0904) 631457
Note : New Family and Disabled Stand to be constructed during 1992/93 season.

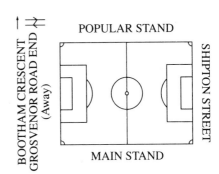

Travelling Supporters Information:

Routes: From North: Take A1 then A59 following York signs. Cross Railway Bridge and turn left (2 miles) into Water End. Turn right at end following City Centre signs for nearly 0.5 mile then turn left into Bootham Crescent; From South: Take A64 and turn left after Buckles Inn on to Outer Ring Road. Turn right onto A19 following City Centre signs for 1.5 miles then turn left into Bootham Crescent; From East: Take Outer Ring Road turning left onto A19 then as South; From West: Take Outer Ring Road turning right on to A19, then as South.

DISABLED INFORMATION

The information shown in this section was provided by the clubs and is as complete as possible. Although the number of spaces for wheelchairs can be very limited, most clubs will endeavour to accommodate wheelchair users even if the spaces have already been filled but, in every case, we advise a telephone enquiry at least 7 days before the game.

Disabled supporters (other than wheelchair users) may experience difficulty in obtaining discretionary 'disabled' entry rates, as some clubs seem to regard wheelchair users alone as qualifying for reduced or free rates where applicable.

A final word of warning - a number of clubs are in the process of revamping their disabled facilities and the information shown below may therefore change for those clubs. Once again, we emphasise that if any points remain unclear, please contact the club in question *at least* 7 days before the game.

ARSENAL FC

WHEELCHAIRS : **Location of Accommodation**: Disabled Section, Lower Tier East Stand
Nº Spaces for Home Fans; Nº Spaces for Away Fans: 20 spaces available in total
Are Helpers Admitted; Nº Admitted: One Helper admitted per Wheelchair. 20 in total.
PRICES : **Prices for Disabled; Prices for Helpers**: Free of Charge
TOILETS : **Location of Disabled Toilets (+ Number)**: 3 in South Stand. One in Lower East 'H' block
BLIND : **Facilities Available**: Commentaries Available
BOOKINGS : **Are Bookings Necessary**: Yes   **CONTACT NUMBER**: (071) 226-0304

ASTON VILLA FC

WHEELCHAIRS : **Location of Accommodation**: Special Section - Trinity Road Stand
Nº Spaces for Home Fans; Nº Spaces for Away Fans: 50 Spaces in total
Are Helpers Admitted; Nº Admitted: By letter of request of disabled - one per disabled fan.
PRICES : **Prices for Disabled; Prices for Helpers**: At Club's discretion for disabled. Helpers full price.
TOILETS : **Location of Disabled Toilets (+ Number)**: One in Trinity Road Stand
BLIND : **Facilities Available**: Commentaries by Arrangement
BOOKINGS : **Are Bookings Necessary**: Yes   **CONTACT NUMBER**: (021) 327-2299

BARNET FC

WHEELCHAIRS : **Location of Accommodation**: Main Stand - Barnet Lane Entrance (Social Club End)
Nº Spaces for Home Fans; Nº Spaces for Away Fans: 12 Spaces in Total
Are Helpers Admitted; Nº Admitted: One helper admitted per wheelchair
PRICES : **Prices for Disabled; Prices for Helpers**: Contact club for details
TOILETS : **Location of Disabled Toilets (+ Number)**: One in Social Club
BLIND : **Facilities Available**: No Special Facilities
BOOKINGS : **Are Bookings Necessary**: Yes   **CONTACT NUMBER**: (081) 441-6932

BARNSLEY FC

WHEELCHAIRS : **Location of Accommodation:** Accommodated in Disabled Stand (Left of Main Stand)
Nº Spaces for Home Fans; Nº Spaces for Away Fans: 55 Spaces in Total
Are Helpers Admitted; Nº Admitted: Yes; Depends on Opponents
PRICES : **Prices for Disabled; Prices for Helpers:** Disabled admitted free. Helpers £5.50
TOILETS : **Location of Disabled Toilets (+ Number):** Adjacent to Disabled Stand
BLIND : **Facilities Available:** Commentaries Available
BOOKINGS : **Are Bookings Necessary:** Usually Not   **CONTACT NUMBER:** (0226) 295363

BIRMINGHAM CITY FC

WHEELCHAIRS : **Location of Accommodation:** Remploy Stand
Nº Spaces for Home Fans; Nº Spaces for Away Fans: Pass Holders (Away Fans please ring)
Are Helpers Admitted; Nº Admitted: One helper admitted per wheelchair
PRICES : **Prices for Disabled; Prices for Helpers:** Free of Charge for each disabled person & helper
TOILETS : **Location of Disabled Toilets (+ Number):** One available in Remploy Stand
BLIND : **Facilities Available:** No Special Facilities
BOOKINGS : **Are Bookings Necessary:** No   **CONTACT NUMBER:** (021) 772-0101

BLACKBURN ROVERS FC

WHEELCHAIRS : **Location of Accommodation:** Disabled Section in Walkersteel Stand
Nº Spaces for Home Fans; Nº Spaces for Away Fans: 26 Spaces for Home fans; 5 for Away
Are Helpers Admitted; Nº Admitted: One helper admitted per disabled supporter
PRICES : **Prices for Disabled; Prices for Helpers:** Free of Charge for both disabled & helpers
TOILETS : **Location of Disabled Toilets (+ Number):** In Disabled Section
BLIND : **Facilities Available:** Commentaries Available by Arrangement for up to 6 people
BOOKINGS : **Are Bookings Necessary:** Yes   **CONTACT NUMBER:** (0254) 55432

BLACKPOOL FC

WHEELCHAIRS : **Location of Accommodation:** In South Paddock
Nº Spaces for Home Fans; Nº Spaces for Away Fans: 12 Spaces in total
Are Helpers Admitted; Nº Admitted: One helper admitted per disabled supporter
PRICES : **Prices for Disabled; Prices for Helpers:** Free of Charge for both disabled & helpers
TOILETS : **Location of Disabled Toilets (+ Number):** None
BLIND : **Facilities Available:** Headphone Commentaries Available in South Stand for three people
BOOKINGS : **Are Bookings Necessary:** Yes   **CONTACT NUMBER:** (0253) 404331

BOLTON WANDERERS FC

WHEELCHAIRS : **Location of Accommodation:** Manchester Road Paddock
Nº Spaces for Home Fans; Nº Spaces for Away Fans: 4 spaces each for Home & Away fans
Are Helpers Admitted; Nº Admitted: One helper admitted per disabled person
PRICES : **Prices for Disabled; Prices for Helpers:** Free of charge for Wheelchairs. Helpers full-price
TOILETS : **Location of Disabled Toilets (+ Number):** One available in Disabled Area
BLIND : **Facilities Available:** No Special Facilities
BOOKINGS : **Are Bookings Necessary:** No   **CONTACT NUMBER:** (0204) 389200

AFC BOURNEMOUTH

WHEELCHAIRS : **Location of Accommodation:** Accommodated by Prior Arrangement - South Stand
Nº Spaces for Home Fans; Nº Spaces for Away Fans: 16 Spaces in total
Are Helpers Admitted; Nº Admitted: One helper admitted per disabled person
PRICES : **Prices for Disabled; Prices for Helpers:** Free of Charge for both disabled & helpers
TOILETS : **Location of Disabled Toilets (+ Number):** One in South Stand - adjacent to Disabled Section
BLIND : **Facilities Available:** No Special Facilities
BOOKINGS : **Are Bookings Necessary:** Yes   **CONTACT NUMBER:** (0202) 395381

BRADFORD CITY FC

WHEELCHAIRS : **Location of Accommodation:** 'A' Block, N & P Stand
Nº Spaces for Home Fans; Nº Spaces for Away Fans: 40 Spaces available in total
Are Helpers Admitted; Nº Admitted: One helper admitted per disabled person
PRICES : **Prices for Disabled; Prices for Helpers:** Both disabled fans and helpers admitted half-price
TOILETS : **Location of Disabled Toilets (+ Number):** One behind disabled section
BLIND : **Facilities Available:** No Special Facilities
BOOKINGS : **Are Bookings Necessary:** Yes   **CONTACT NUMBER:** (0274) 306062

BRENTFORD FC

WHEELCHAIRS : **Location of Accommodation**: Disabled Section - Brook Road End
Nº **Spaces for Home Fans**; Nº **Spaces for Away Fans**: 30 spaces available in total
Are Helpers Admitted; Nº **Admitted**: One helper admitted per disabled person
PRICES : **Prices for Disabled**; **Prices for Helpers**: Free of charge for both the disabled and helpers.
TOILETS : **Location of Disabled Toilets (+ Number)**: One each (male & female) Braemar Road
BLIND : **Facilities Available**: Commentaries Available in Braemar Road Stand
BOOKINGS : **Are Bookings Necessary**: No   **CONTACT NUMBER**: (081) 560-6062

BRIGHTON & HOVE ALBION FC

WHEELCHAIRS : **Location of Accommodation**: Disabled Section - S.W. Corner of Ground
Nº **Spaces for Home Fans**; Nº **Spaces for Away Fans**: 30 Spaces in total
Are Helpers Admitted; Nº **Admitted**: One helper admitted per disabled person. Seats nearby
PRICES : **Prices for Disabled**; **Prices for Helpers**: Disabled free of charge - helpers £5.00
TOILETS : **Location of Disabled Toilets (+ Number)**: One in the disabled section
BLIND : **Facilities Available**: Commentaries Available in West Stand
BOOKINGS : **Are Bookings Necessary**: Yes   **CONTACT NUMBER**: (0273) 778855

BRISTOL CITY FC

WHEELCHAIRS : **Location of Accommodation**: Accommodated at Pitchside
Nº **Spaces for Home Fans**; Nº **Spaces for Away Fans**: Limited Number - please apply early
Are Helpers Admitted; Nº **Admitted**: One helper admitted per disabled person
PRICES : **Prices for Disabled**; **Prices for Helpers**: Free of charge for both the disabled & helpers
TOILETS : **Location of Disabled Toilets (+ Number)**: 2 toilets available
BLIND : **Facilities Available**: Commentaries Available (Please contact club for further information)
BOOKINGS : **Are Bookings Necessary**: Yes   **CONTACT NUMBER**: (0272) 632812

BRISTOL ROVERS FC

WHEELCHAIRS : **Location of Accommodation**: Accommodated in Family Stand
Nº **Spaces for Home Fans**; Nº **Spaces for Away Fans**: 14 Spaces available in total
Are Helpers Admitted; Nº **Admitted**: One helper admitted per disabled supporter
PRICES : **Prices for Disabled**; **Prices for Helpers**: Free of charge for both the disabled & helpers
TOILETS : **Location of Disabled Toilets (+ Number)**: One available in Family Stand
BLIND : **Facilities Available**: Commentaries Available by Arrangement (please contact club early)
BOOKINGS : **Are Bookings Necessary**: Yes   **CONTACT NUMBER**: (0272) 352508

BURNLEY FC

WHEELCHAIRS : **Location of Accommodation**: In Front of Bob Lord Stand
Nº **Spaces for Home Fans**; Nº **Spaces for Away Fans**: Limited Number of Spaces
Are Helpers Admitted; Nº **Admitted**: One helper admitted per disabled supporter
PRICES : **Prices for Disabled**; **Prices for Helpers**: Childrens prices for disabled. Full-price for helpers
TOILETS : **Location of Disabled Toilets (+ Number)**: None
BLIND : **Facilities Available**: No Special Facilities
BOOKINGS : **Are Bookings Necessary**: No   **CONTACT NUMBER**: (0282) 27777

BURY FC

WHEELCHAIRS : **Location of Accommodation**: Accommodated between the Cemetery End & South Stand
Nº **Spaces for Home Fans**; Nº **Spaces for Away Fans**: Not Specified
Are Helpers Admitted; Nº **Admitted**: Helpers admitted - unspecified number
PRICES : **Prices for Disabled**; **Prices for Helpers**: Disabled half-price. Helpers full-price
TOILETS : **Location of Disabled Toilets (+ Number)**: None
BLIND : **Facilities Available**: Radio Commentary in Press Box
BOOKINGS : **Are Bookings Necessary**: Yes   **CONTACT NUMBER**: (061) 764-4881

CAMBRIDGE UNITED FC

WHEELCHAIRS : **Location of Accommodation**: In Disabled Section - in front of Main Stand
Nº **Spaces for Home Fans**; Nº **Spaces for Away Fans**: 12 Spaces available in total
Are Helpers Admitted; Nº **Admitted**: One helper admitted per disabled supporter
PRICES : **Prices for Disabled**; **Prices for Helpers**: Free of Charge for the disabled. Half-price for helpers
TOILETS : **Location of Disabled Toilets (+ Number)**: None
BLIND : **Facilities Available**: No Special Facilities
BOOKINGS : **Are Bookings Necessary**: Yes   **CONTACT NUMBER**: (0223) 241237

CARDIFF CITY FC

WHEELCHAIRS : Location of Accommodation: Accommodated in Canton Stand/Popular Bank Corner
Nº Spaces for Home Fans; Nº Spaces for Away Fans: 20 spaces each for Home & Away
Are Helpers Admitted; Nº Admitted: One helper admitted per disabled supporter
PRICES : Prices for Disabled; Prices for Helpers: Please phone for details
TOILETS : Location of Disabled Toilets (+ Number): None
BLIND : Facilities Available: No Special Facilities
BOOKINGS : Are Bookings Necessary: No CONTACT NUMBER: (0222) 398636

CARLISLE UNITED FC

WHEELCHAIRS : Location of Accommodation: Disabled Section (in front of paddock) by Prior Arrangement
Nº Spaces for Home Fans; Nº Spaces for Away Fans: Limited Number of Spaces
Are Helpers Admitted; Nº Admitted: One helper admitted per disabled supporter
PRICES : Prices for Disabled; Prices for Helpers: Will advise when booking
TOILETS : Location of Disabled Toilets (+ Number): None
BLIND : Facilities Available: Commentaries Available
BOOKINGS : Are Bookings Necessary: Yes CONTACT NUMBER: (0228) 26237

CHARLTON ATHLETIC FC

WHEELCHAIRS : Location of Accommodation: East Stand
Nº Spaces for Home Fans; Nº Spaces for Away Fans: 50 spaces in total
Are Helpers Admitted; Nº Admitted: Yes - up to 25 helpers are admitted
PRICES : Prices for Disabled; Prices for Helpers: Free of charge for disabled, helpers charged £5.00
TOILETS : Location of Disabled Toilets (+ Number): In East Stand
BLIND : Facilities Available: No Special Facilities
BOOKINGS : Are Bookings Necessary: Yes CONTACT NUMBER: (081) 293-4567

CHELSEA FC

WHEELCHAIRS : Location of Accommodation: Accommodated in East Stand Concourse
Nº Spaces for Home Fans; Nº Spaces for Away Fans: Approximately 40 spaces in total
Are Helpers Admitted; Nº Admitted: One helper admitted per disabled supporter
PRICES : Prices for Disabled; Prices for Helpers: Free of charge for disabled. Full price for helpers
TOILETS : Location of Disabled Toilets (+ Number): East Stand Concourse: 1 male and 1 female
BLIND : Facilities Available: No Special Facilities
BOOKINGS : Are Bookings Necessary: Yes CONTACT NUMBER: (071) 385-5545

CHESTER CITY FC

WHEELCHAIRS : Location of Accommodation: West Stand
Nº Spaces for Home Fans; Nº Spaces for Away Fans: Number not specified (Ample Room)
Are Helpers Admitted; Nº Admitted: One helper admitted per disabled person
PRICES : Prices for Disabled; Prices for Helpers: Free of charge for the disabled. Helpers normal prices
TOILETS : Location of Disabled Toilets (+ Number): Available in West Stand
BLIND : Facilities Available: No Special Facilities - But phone for further information
BOOKINGS : Are Bookings Necessary: Yes CONTACT NUMBER: (0244) 371376

CHESTERFIELD FC

WHEELCHAIRS : Location of Accommodation: Below Saltergate Wing Stand
Nº Spaces for Home Fans; Nº Spaces for Away Fans: 20 Spaces available in total
Are Helpers Admitted; Nº Admitted: One helper admitted per disabled supporter
PRICES : Prices for Disabled; Prices for Helpers: Free of charge for the disabled. Helpers £5.50
TOILETS : Location of Disabled Toilets (+ Number): One available underneath Main Stand
BLIND : Facilities Available: No Special Facilities
BOOKINGS : Are Bookings Necessary: No CONTACT NUMBER: (0246) 209765

COLCHESTER UNITED FC

WHEELCHAIRS : Location of Accommodation: In front of Main Stand
Nº Spaces for Home Fans; Nº Spaces for Away Fans: Limited Number
Are Helpers Admitted; Nº Admitted: One helper admitted per disabled person
PRICES : Prices for Disabled; Prices for Helpers: Free for the disabled. Helpers charged seating prices
TOILETS : Location of Disabled Toilets (+ Number): None
BLIND : Facilities Available: Commentaries available for 6 people
BOOKINGS : Are Bookings Necessary: Yes CONTACT NUMBER: (0206) 574042

COVENTRY CITY FC

WHEELCHAIRS : **Location of Accommodation :** Disabled Section in Clock Stand
Nº Spaces for Home Fans; Nº Spaces for Away Fans : 24 spaces in total
Are Helpers Admitted; Nº Admitted : Up to 47 helpers admitted
PRICES : **Prices for Disabled; Prices for Helpers :** £4.00 for the disabled. £8.00 for helpers
TOILETS : **Location of Disabled Toilets (+ Number) :** 2 - adjacent to disabled area
BLIND : **Facilities Available :** No Special Facilities
BOOKINGS : **Are Bookings Necessary :** Yes **CONTACT NUMBER :** (0203) 225545

CREWE ALEXANDRA FC

WHEELCHAIRS : **Location of Accommodation :** Corner of Popular Side/Family Area
Nº Spaces for Home Fans; Nº Spaces for Away Fans : Approximately 20 spaces available
Are Helpers Admitted; Nº Admitted : One helper admitted per disabled supporter
PRICES : **Prices for Disabled; Prices for Helpers :** Free of Charge for the disabled. Helpers full-price
TOILETS : **Location of Disabled Toilets (+ Number) :** Planned within disabled area
BLIND : **Facilities Available :** Commentaries Available
BOOKINGS : **Are Bookings Necessary :** Yes **CONTACT NUMBER :** (0270) 213014

CRYSTAL PALACE FC

WHEELCHAIRS : **Location of Accommodation :** In Disabled Section - Arthur Wait Stand (Park Road Entrance)
Nº Spaces for Home Fans; Nº Spaces for Away Fans : 28 spaces for home fans; 4 for away
Are Helpers Admitted; Nº Admitted : One helper admitted per wheelchair
PRICES : **Prices for Disabled; Prices for Helpers :** Disabled Free of Charge . Helpers pay full-price.
TOILETS : **Location of Disabled Toilets (+ Number) :** Located in disabled section
BLIND : **Facilities Available :** Commentaries Available - 4 places available
BOOKINGS : **Are Bookings Necessary :** Yes **CONTACT NUMBER :** (081) 653-4462

DARLINGTON FC

WHEELCHAIRS : **Location of Accommodation :** Accommodated in Disabled Section - East Stand
Nº Spaces for Home Fans; Nº Spaces for Away Fans : 20 spaces each for home & away fans
Are Helpers Admitted; Nº Admitted : One helper admitted with each disabled person
PRICES : **Prices for Disabled; Prices for Helpers :** £2.50 for the disabled. £5.00 for helpers
TOILETS : **Location of Disabled Toilets (+ Number) :** None
BLIND : **Facilities Available :** No Special Facilities
BOOKINGS : **Are Bookings Necessary :** No **CONTACT NUMBER :** (0325) 465097

DERBY COUNTY FC

WHEELCHAIRS : **Location of Accommodation :** Accommodated in Disabled Section - Normanton End
Nº Spaces for Home Fans; Nº Spaces for Away Fans : 80 spaces available in total
Are Helpers Admitted; Nº Admitted : One helper admitted per disabled person
PRICES : **Prices for Disabled; Prices for Helpers :** Free of charge for both the disabled and helpers
TOILETS : **Location of Disabled Toilets (+ Number) :** Available in Disabled Section
BLIND : **Facilities Available :** Commentaries available in Disabled Viewing Gallery
BOOKINGS : **Are Bookings Necessary :** Yes **CONTACT NUMBER :** (0332) 40105

DONCASTER ROVERS FC

WHEELCHAIRS : **Location of Accommodation :** Accommodated in Disabled Section - 'A' Block
Nº Spaces for Home Fans; Nº Spaces for Away Fans : Limited number of spaces available
Are Helpers Admitted; Nº Admitted : One helper admitted per wheelchair
PRICES : **Prices for Disabled; Prices for Helpers :** Free of charge for both the disabled & the helpers
TOILETS : **Location of Disabled Toilets (+ Number) :** None
BLIND : **Facilities Available :** No Special Facilities
BOOKINGS : **Are Bookings Necessary :** Yes **CONTACT NUMBER :** (0302) 539441

EVERTON FC

WHEELCHAIRS : **Location of Accommodation :** Disabled Section - Bullens Road
Nº Spaces for Home Fans; Nº Spaces for Away Fans : 25 spaces for home fans; 5 for away
Are Helpers Admitted; Nº Admitted : One helper admitted with each wheelchair
PRICES : **Prices for Disabled; Prices for Helpers :** Free for the disabled. £9.50 - £11.50 for helpers
TOILETS : **Location of Disabled Toilets (+ Number) :** One in Disabled Section
BLIND : **Facilities Available :** Seats with commentaries available
BOOKINGS : **Are Bookings Necessary :** Yes **CONTACT NUMBER :** (051) 523-6666

EXETER CITY FC

WHEELCHAIRS :   **Location of Accommodation**: In front of Main Grandstand
                    Nº Spaces for Home Fans; Nº Spaces for Away Fans: Limited Number
                    Are Helpers Admitted; Nº Admitted: One helper admitted per wheelchair
PRICES :   **Prices for Disabled; Prices for Helpers**: £5.00 for the disabled. £8.00 per helper
TOILETS :   **Location of Disabled Toilets (+ Number)**: None
BLIND :   **Facilities Available**: No Special Facilities
BOOKINGS :   **Are Bookings Necessary**: Yes   **CONTACT NUMBER**: (0392) 54073

FULHAM FC

WHEELCHAIRS :   **Location of Accommodation**: Disabled Section - alongside Miller Stand Touchline
                    Nº Spaces for Home Fans; Nº Spaces for Away Fans: 20 spaces in total
                    Are Helpers Admitted; Nº Admitted: One helper admitted per disabled person
PRICES :   **Prices for Disabled; Prices for Helpers**: Free of charge for the disabled. Helpers £6.00
TOILETS :   **Location of Disabled Toilets (+ Number)**: None
BLIND :   **Facilities Available**: Commentaries Available by Prior Arrangement
BOOKINGS :   **Are Bookings Necessary**: Yes   **CONTACT NUMBER**: (071) 736-6561

GILLINGHAM FC

WHEELCHAIRS :   **Location of Accommodation**: Disabled Section - adjacent to Main Stand (Redfern Avenue)
                    Nº Spaces for Home Fans; Nº Spaces for Away Fans: 20 spaces available in total
                    Are Helpers Admitted; Nº Admitted: One helper admitted per disabled supporter
PRICES :   **Prices for Disabled; Prices for Helpers**: Both helpers and disabled pay normal ground prices
TOILETS :   **Location of Disabled Toilets (+ Number)**: None
BLIND :   **Facilities Available**: No Special Facilities
BOOKINGS :   **Are Bookings Necessary**: Preferred   **CONTACT NUMBER**: (0634) 851462

GRIMSBY TOWN FC

WHEELCHAIRS :   **Location of Accommodation**: Accommodated in Disabled Section - Main Stand
                    Nº Spaces for Home Fans; Nº Spaces for Away Fans: 50 spaces - Home fans only
                    Are Helpers Admitted; Nº Admitted: Membership restricted to Handicapped Supp. Club -
PRICES :   **Prices for Disabled; Prices for Helpers**: Maximum of 50
TOILETS :   **Location of Disabled Toilets (+ Number)**: In Disabled Section
BLIND :   **Facilities Available**: Commentaries Available in Disabled Section
BOOKINGS :   **Are Bookings Necessary**: Seasonal only **CONTACT NUMBER**: (0472) 696904

HALIFAX TOWN FC

WHEELCHAIRS :   **Location of Accommodation**: Accommodated in Disabled Section - Family Stand
                    Nº Spaces for Home Fans; Nº Spaces for Away Fans: 10 spaces in total
                    Are Helpers Admitted; Nº Admitted: Yes
PRICES :   **Prices for Disabled; Prices for Helpers**: 1 disabled & 1 helper costs £8. Extra helpers £7 each
TOILETS :   **Location of Disabled Toilets (+ Number)**: At end of ramp from Stand
BLIND :   **Facilities Available**: No Special Facilities
BOOKINGS :   **Are Bookings Necessary**: No   **CONTACT NUMBER**: (0422) 353423

HARTLEPOOL UNITED FC

WHEELCHAIRS :   **Location of Accommodation**: Disabled Section - Mill House side of Ground
                    Nº Spaces for Home Fans; Nº Spaces for Away Fans: Total of 20 spaces available
                    Are Helpers Admitted; Nº Admitted: One helper admitted with each disabled supporter
PRICES :   **Prices for Disabled; Prices for Helpers**: £4.00 for the disabled. £6.00 for helpers
TOILETS :   **Location of Disabled Toilets (+ Number)**: None
BLIND :   **Facilities Available**: Commentaries Available
BOOKINGS :   **Are Bookings Necessary**: No   **CONTACT NUMBER**: (0429) 272584

HEREFORD UNITED FC

WHEELCHAIRS :   **Location of Accommodation**: Accommodated in Disabled Section - Edgar Street Side
                    Nº Spaces for Home Fans; Nº Spaces for Away Fans: 10 spaces in total
                    Are Helpers Admitted; Nº Admitted: One helper admitted per disabled supporter
PRICES :   **Prices for Disabled; Prices for Helpers**: £4.00 each for both the disabled and helpers
TOILETS :   **Location of Disabled Toilets (+ Number)**: None
BLIND :   **Facilities Available**: No Special Facilities
BOOKINGS :   **Are Bookings Necessary**: No   **CONTACT NUMBER**: (0432) 276666

HUDDERSFIELD TOWN FC

WHEELCHAIRS : **Location of Accommodation**: Accommodated in Disabled Section - Main Stand
Nº Spaces for Home Fans; Nº Spaces for Away Fans: 30 spaces available in total
Are Helpers Admitted; Nº Admitted: One helper admitted per wheelchair
PRICES : **Prices for Disabled; Prices for Helpers**: Free of charge for the disabled. £3.50 per helper.
TOILETS : **Location of Disabled Toilets (+ Number)**: One adjacent to disabled section
BLIND : **Facilities Available**: No Special Facilities
BOOKINGS : **Are Bookings Necessary**: Yes   **CONTACT NUMBER**: (0484) 420335

HULL CITY FC

WHEELCHAIRS : **Location of Accommodation**: Accommodated in Disabled Enclosure - South East Corner
Nº Spaces for Home Fans; Nº Spaces for Away Fans: Approximately 20 spaces in total
Are Helpers Admitted; Nº Admitted: One helper admitted per disabled person
PRICES : **Prices for Disabled; Prices for Helpers**: Free of charge for the disabled. £6.00 per helper
TOILETS : **Location of Disabled Toilets (+ Number)**: One toilet situated within disabled enclosure
BLIND : **Facilities Available**: Commentaries Available
BOOKINGS : **Are Bookings Necessary**: No   **CONTACT NUMBER**: (0482) 51119

IPSWICH TOWN FC

WHEELCHAIRS : **Location of Accommodation**: Accommodated in Disabled Section - Churchmans Stand
Nº Spaces for Home Fans; Nº Spaces for Away Fans: 50 spaces available in total
Are Helpers Admitted; Nº Admitted: One helper admitted per disabled person
PRICES : **Prices for Disabled; Prices for Helpers**: Free of charge for the disabled. £7.00 for helpers
TOILETS : **Location of Disabled Toilets (+ Number)**: Adjacent to Stand
BLIND : **Facilities Available**: Commentaries Available
BOOKINGS : **Are Bookings Necessary**: Yes   **CONTACT NUMBER**: (0473) 219211

LEEDS UNITED FC

WHEELCHAIRS : **Location of Accommodation**: Accommodated in Disabled Section - West Stand
Nº Spaces for Home Fans; Nº Spaces for Away Fans: 24 spaces for wheelchairs in total
Are Helpers Admitted; Nº Admitted: One helper admitted per disabled person
PRICES : **Prices for Disabled; Prices for Helpers**: Free of charge for the disabled. £9.00 for helpers
TOILETS : **Location of Disabled Toilets (+ Number)**: One adjacent to the Disabled Section
BLIND : **Facilities Available**: Commentaries via Headphones in West Stand
BOOKINGS : **Are Bookings Necessary**: Yes   **CONTACT NUMBER**: (0532) 716037

LEICESTER CITY FC

WHEELCHAIRS : **Location of Accommodation**: Family Club Area
Nº Spaces for Home Fans; Nº Spaces for Away Fans: Total of 8 spaces available
Are Helpers Admitted; Nº Admitted: One helper admitted per disabled person
PRICES : **Prices for Disabled; Prices for Helpers**: Free of charge for the disabled. £7.50 for helpers
TOILETS : **Location of Disabled Toilets (+ Number)**: None at present
BLIND : **Facilities Available**: No Special Facilities at present
BOOKINGS : **Are Bookings Necessary**: Yes   **CONTACT NUMBER**: (0533) 555000

LEYTON ORIENT FC

WHEELCHAIRS : **Location of Accommodation**: Accommodated in Disabled Section - North Terrace
Nº Spaces for Home Fans; Nº Spaces for Away Fans: 12 spaces available in total
Are Helpers Admitted; Nº Admitted: One helper admitted per disabled supporter
PRICES : **Prices for Disabled; Prices for Helpers**: Free of charge for both the disabled and helpers
TOILETS : **Location of Disabled Toilets (+ Number)**: One available near Disabled Section
BLIND : **Facilities Available**: No Special Facilities
BOOKINGS : **Are Bookings Necessary**: Yes   **CONTACT NUMBER**: (081) 539-2223

LINCOLN CITY FC

WHEELCHAIRS : **Location of Accommodation**: Accommodated - Adjacent to Turnstile 1
Nº Spaces for Home Fans; Nº Spaces for Away Fans: 62 spaces available in total
Are Helpers Admitted; Nº Admitted: One helper admitted per disabled supporter
PRICES : **Prices for Disabled; Prices for Helpers**: Free of charge for both the disabled and helpers.
TOILETS : **Location of Disabled Toilets (+ Number)**: Several adjacent to disabled accommodation
BLIND : **Facilities Available**: No Special facilities
BOOKINGS : **Are Bookings Necessary**: Yes   **CONTACT NUMBER**: (0522) 510263

LIVERPOOL FC

WHEELCHAIRS : **Location of Accommodation**: Accommodated in Disabled Section - Paddock Enclosure
Nº Spaces for Home Fans; Nº Spaces for Away Fans: 16 spaces for home. None for away.
Are Helpers Admitted; Nº Admitted: Up to 30 helpers are admitted
PRICES : **Prices for Disabled; Prices for Helpers**: £3.00 per disabled person. £12 or £13 per helper
TOILETS : **Location of Disabled Toilets (+ Number)**: One in the Paddock
BLIND : **Facilities Available**: Commentaries Available in Disabled Section
BOOKINGS : **Are Bookings Necessary**: Yes **CONTACT NUMBER** : (051) 709-3654

LUTON TOWN FC

WHEELCHAIRS : **Location of Accommodation**: In Main Stand
Nº Spaces for Home Fans; Nº Spaces for Away Fans: 15 spaces available in total
Are Helpers Admitted; Nº Admitted: One helper admitted per disabled person
PRICES : **Prices for Disabled; Prices for Helpers**: Free of charge for both disabled and helpers
TOILETS : **Location of Disabled Toilets (+ Number)**: One adjacent to the disabled area
BLIND : **Facilities Available**: Commentaries Available
BOOKINGS : **Are Bookings Necessary**: Yes **CONTACT NUMBER** : (0582) 411622

MAIDSTONE UNITED FC

WHEELCHAIRS : **Location of Accommodation**: Accommodated - Side of Main Stand
Nº Spaces for Home Fans; Nº Spaces for Away Fans: 15 spaces each for home & away fans
Are Helpers Admitted; Nº Admitted: One helper admitted per disabled person
PRICES : **Prices for Disabled; Prices for Helpers**: Free of charge for the disabled. £5.00 for helpers
TOILETS : **Location of Disabled Toilets (+ Number)**: One toilet in Main Stand
BLIND : **Facilities Available**: No Special Facilities
BOOKINGS : **Are Bookings Necessary**: Yes **CONTACT NUMBER** : (0622) 754403

MANCHESTER CITY FC

WHEELCHAIRS : **Location of Accommodation**: The Platt Lane Family Stand to be built
Nº Spaces for Home Fans; Nº Spaces for Away Fans: will include a Disabled Section.
Are Helpers Admitted; Nº Admitted: No disabled toilets will be available
PRICES : **Prices for Disabled; Prices for Helpers**: until February 1993.
TOILETS : **Location of Disabled Toilets (+ Number)**: Please phone for other information.
BLIND : **Facilities Available**: No Special Facilities
BOOKINGS : **Are Bookings Necessary**: Yes **CONTACT NUMBER** : (061) 226-1191

MANCHESTER UNITED FC

WHEELCHAIRS : **Location of Accommodation**: Disabled Section - In front of 'L' Stand ?
Nº Spaces for Home Fans; Nº Spaces for Away Fans: 32 spaces available in total
Are Helpers Admitted; Nº Admitted: One helper admitted per disabled fan
PRICES : **Prices for Disabled; Prices for Helpers**: Free of Charge for both disabled & helpers
TOILETS : **Location of Disabled Toilets (+ Number)**: Located near Disabled Section
BLIND : **Facilities Available**: Commentaries Available
BOOKINGS : **Are Bookings Necessary**: Yes **CONTACT NUMBER** : (061) 872-1661

MANSFIELD TOWN FC

WHEELCHAIRS : **Location of Accommodation**: Accommodated - North End of Bishop Street Terrace
Nº Spaces for Home Fans; Nº Spaces for Away Fans: 40 spaces available in total
Are Helpers Admitted; Nº Admitted: Yes
PRICES : **Prices for Disabled; Prices for Helpers**: Free of charge for the disabled. Helpers full-price
TOILETS : **Location of Disabled Toilets (+ Number)**: Adjacent to terrace
BLIND : **Facilities Available**: No Special Facilities
BOOKINGS : **Are Bookings Necessary**: Not Usually **CONTACT NUMBER** : (0623) 23567

MIDDLESBROUGH FC

WHEELCHAIRS : **Location of Accommodation**: Accommodated in North East Corner
Nº Spaces for Home Fans; Nº Spaces for Away Fans: 20 spaces available in total
Are Helpers Admitted; Nº Admitted: One helper admitted per disabled person
PRICES : **Prices for Disabled; Prices for Helpers**: £3.00 per disabled person, £6.00 per helper
TOILETS : **Location of Disabled Toilets (+ Number)**: One available in North East Corner
BLIND : **Facilities Available**: Commentaries Available
BOOKINGS : **Are Bookings Necessary**: Yes **CONTACT NUMBER** : (0642) 826664

MILLWALL FC

WHEELCHAIRS : **Location of Accommodation:** Accommodated in Disabled Section - South Stand
Nº **Spaces for Home Fans;** Nº **Spaces for Away Fans:** 25 spaces available in total
Are Helpers Admitted; Nº **Admitted:** One helper admitted per disabled person
PRICES : **Prices for Disabled; Prices for Helpers:** Free of charge for both the disabled and helpers
TOILETS : **Location of Disabled Toilets (+ Number):** 2 toilets available in disabled area
BLIND : **Facilities Available:** No Special Facilities
BOOKINGS : **Are Bookings Necessary:** Yes   **CONTACT NUMBER:** (071) 639-3143

NEWCASTLE UNITED FC

WHEELCHAIRS : **Location of Accommodation:** Accommodated in Disabled Section - Leazes Terrace 'F' Section
Nº **Spaces for Home Fans;** Nº **Spaces for Away Fans:** 30 for Home fans. Limited for Away
Are Helpers Admitted; Nº **Admitted:** One helper admitted per disabled supporter
PRICES : **Prices for Disabled; Prices for Helpers:** £2.00 for disabled, £5.00 for helpers (1991/92 prices)
TOILETS : **Location of Disabled Toilets (+ Number):** Located by Disabled Section Entrance
BLIND : **Facilities Available:** Facilities for 20 blind supporters with Match Commentaries
BOOKINGS : **Are Bookings Necessary:** Yes   **CONTACT NUMBER:** (091) 232-8361

NORTHAMPTON TOWN FC

WHEELCHAIRS : **Location of Accommodation:** Accommodated on Cricket Pitch Side
Nº **Spaces for Home Fans;** Nº **Spaces for Away Fans:** 15 spaces available in total
Are Helpers Admitted; Nº **Admitted:** One helper admitted per disabled supporter
PRICES : **Prices for Disabled; Prices for Helpers:** Free of charge for the disabled. Helpers full-price
TOILETS : **Location of Disabled Toilets (+ Number):** None
BLIND : **Facilities Available:** No Special Facilities
BOOKINGS : **Are Bookings Necessary:** Yes   **CONTACT NUMBER:** (0604) 234100

NORWICH CITY FC

WHEELCHAIRS : **Location of Accommodation:** South Stand/River End corner (Glazed & Heated)
Nº **Spaces for Home Fans;** Nº **Spaces for Away Fans:** 34 spaces for home fans; 6 for away
Are Helpers Admitted; Nº **Admitted:** One helper admitted for each disabled person
PRICES : **Prices for Disabled; Prices for Helpers:** Free of charge for both the disabled and helpers
TOILETS : **Location of Disabled Toilets (+ Number):** One within disabled enclosure
BLIND : **Facilities Available:** No Special Facilities
BOOKINGS : **Are Bookings Necessary:** Yes   **CONTACT NUMBER:** (0603) 761661

NOTTINGHAM FOREST FC

WHEELCHAIRS : **Location of Accommodation:** Disabled Section - In front of Executive Stand
Nº **Spaces for Home Fans;** Nº **Spaces for Away Fans:** 50 spaces available in total
Are Helpers Admitted; Nº **Admitted:** One helper admitted per disabled person
PRICES : **Prices for Disabled; Prices for Helpers:** Free of charge for the disabled. £10.00 for helpers
TOILETS : **Location of Disabled Toilets (+ Number):** Available in Executive Stand
BLIND : **Facilities Available:** No Special Facilities
BOOKINGS : **Are Bookings Necessary:** Yes   **CONTACT NUMBER:** (0602) 813801

NOTTS COUNTY FC

WHEELCHAIRS : **Location of Accommodation:** Disabled Section - County Road/Meadow Lane End Corner
Nº **Spaces for Home Fans;** Nº **Spaces for Away Fans:** 25 spaces in total
Are Helpers Admitted; Nº **Admitted:** One helper admitted per disabled supporter
PRICES : **Prices for Disabled; Prices for Helpers:** Free of charge for the disabled. £7.00 for helpers
TOILETS : **Location of Disabled Toilets (+ Number):** Next to disabled area
BLIND : **Facilities Available:** No Special Facilities
BOOKINGS : **Are Bookings Necessary:** Yes   **CONTACT NUMBER:** (0602) 861155/850632

OLDHAM ATHLETIC FC

WHEELCHAIRS : **Location of Accommodation:** Accommodated in Disabled Section - Lookers Paddock
Nº **Spaces for Home Fans;** Nº **Spaces for Away Fans:** 24 spaces available in total
Are Helpers Admitted; Nº **Admitted:** One helper admitted per disabled supporter
PRICES : **Prices for Disabled; Prices for Helpers:** Free of charge for the disabled. Full-prices for helpers
TOILETS : **Location of Disabled Toilets (+ Number):** Available in Lookers Paddock
BLIND : **Facilities Available:** Commentaries Available
BOOKINGS : **Are Bookings Necessary:** Yes   **CONTACT NUMBER:** (061) 624-4972

OXFORD UNITED FC

WHEELCHAIRS :   **Location of Accommodation:** Disabled Section - Beech Road Corner
     Nº Spaces for Home Fans; Nº Spaces for Away Fans: 25 spaces available in total
     Are Helpers Admitted; Nº Admitted: One helper admitted per disabled person (25 max.)
PRICES :   **Prices for Disabled; Prices for Helpers:** £5.00 for the disabled. Helpers normal prices
TOILETS :   **Location of Disabled Toilets (+ Number):** One available in Beech Road Corner
BLIND :   **Facilities Available:** No Special Facilities
BOOKINGS :   **Are Bookings Necessary:** Yes   **CONTACT NUMBER:** (0865) 61503

PETERBOROUGH UNITED FC

WHEELCHAIRS :   **Location of Accommodation:** Accommodated in Disabled Area - Left Side of Main Stand
     Nº Spaces for Home Fans; Nº Spaces for Away Fans: 12 spaces available in total
     Are Helpers Admitted; Nº Admitted: One helper admitted per disabled supporter
PRICES :   **Prices for Disabled; Prices for Helpers:** £3.50 for the disabled and helpers (1991/92 prices)
TOILETS :   **Location of Disabled Toilets (+ Number):** None
BLIND :   **Facilities Available:** No Special Facilities
BOOKINGS :   **Are Bookings Necessary:** Yes   **CONTACT NUMBER:** (0733) 63947

PLYMOUTH ARGYLE FC

WHEELCHAIRS :   **Location of Accommodation:** Accommodated in Disabled Section in Devonport End
     Nº Spaces for Home Fans; Nº Spaces for Away Fans: Total of 60 spaces available
     Are Helpers Admitted; Nº Admitted: One helper admitted per disabled person
PRICES :   **Prices for Disabled; Prices for Helpers:** Free of charge for the disabled. £5.50 for helpers
TOILETS :   **Location of Disabled Toilets (+ Number):** Adjacent to disabled section
BLIND :   **Facilities Available:** Commentaries Available
BOOKINGS :   **Are Bookings Necessary:** Yes   **CONTACT NUMBER:** (0752) 562561

PORTSMOUTH FC

WHEELCHAIRS :   **Location of Accommodation:** Accommodated in Disabled Section - Fratton Road End
     Nº Spaces for Home Fans; Nº Spaces for Away Fans: Limited number of spaces available
     Are Helpers Admitted; Nº Admitted: One helper admitted per disabled supporter
PRICES :   **Prices for Disabled; Prices for Helpers:** Free of charge for both the disabled and helpers
TOILETS :   **Location of Disabled Toilets (+ Number):** One in disabled section
BLIND :   **Facilities Available:** No Special Facilities
BOOKINGS :   **Are Bookings Necessary:** Yes   **CONTACT NUMBER:** (0705) 731204

PORT VALE FC

WHEELCHAIRS :   **Location of Accommodation:** Disabled Section - Lorne Street/Hamil Road Corner
     Nº Spaces for Home Fans; Nº Spaces for Away Fans: 72 spaces available in total
     Are Helpers Admitted; Nº Admitted: One helper admitted per disabled person on request
PRICES :   **Prices for Disabled; Prices for Helpers:** £3.50 for the disabled, £6.50 for helpers
TOILETS :   **Location of Disabled Toilets (+ Number):** One available in Disabled Section
BLIND :   **Facilities Available:** Commentaries are available - Please contact Club
BOOKINGS :   **Are Bookings Necessary:** Yes   **CONTACT NUMBER:** (0782) 814134

PRESTON NORTH END FC

WHEELCHAIRS :   **Location of Accommodation:** Perimeter track in front of West Stand Paddocks (Deepdale Rd.)
     Nº Spaces for Home Fans; Nº Spaces for Away Fans: 20 spaces available in total
     Are Helpers Admitted; Nº Admitted: Usually one helper per wheelchair. More if necessary.
PRICES :   **Prices for Disabled; Prices for Helpers:** Disabled plus one helper free. Extra helpers £4.50 ?
TOILETS :   **Location of Disabled Toilets (+ Number):** One available at Invalid Entrance - Deepdale Road
BLIND :   **Facilities Available:** No Special Facilities
BOOKINGS :   **Are Bookings Necessary:** Sometimes   **CONTACT NUMBER:** (0772) 795919

QUEENS PARK RANGERS FC

WHEELCHAIRS :   **Location of Accommodation:** In Wheelchair enclosure - Left Side of Ellerslie Road Stand
     Nº Spaces for Home Fans; Nº Spaces for Away Fans: Total of 20 spaces available.
     Are Helpers Admitted; Nº Admitted: One helper admitted per wheelchair
PRICES :   **Prices for Disabled; Prices for Helpers:** Free of charge for both the disabled and helpers
TOILETS :   **Location of Disabled Toilets (+ Number):** None
BLIND :   **Facilities Available:** No Special Facilities
BOOKINGS :   **Are Bookings Necessary:** Yes   **CONTACT NUMBER:** Please contact in writing

READING FC

WHEELCHAIRS : **Location of Accommodation :** Accommodated in Front Row 'E' Stand
Nº Spaces for Home Fans; Nº Spaces for Away Fans : 10 spaces available in total
Are Helpers Admitted; Nº Admitted : Yes
PRICES : **Prices for Disabled; Prices for Helpers :** Free of charge for the disabled. £6.00 per helper
TOILETS : **Location of Disabled Toilets (+ Number) :** One adjacent to stand
BLIND : **Facilities Available :** No Special Facilities
BOOKINGS : **Are Bookings Necessary :** Yes   **CONTACT NUMBER :** (0734) 507878

ROCHDALE FC

WHEELCHAIRS : **Location of Accommodation :**   New Stand in Course of Construction
Nº Spaces for Home Fans; Nº Spaces for Away Fans : - details not yet finalised
Are Helpers Admitted; Nº Admitted : One helper admitted per disabled person
PRICES : **Prices for Disabled; Prices for Helpers :** Free of charge for the disabled. £1.50 per helper
TOILETS : **Location of Disabled Toilets (+ Number) :** None
BLIND : **Facilities Available :** No Special Facilities
BOOKINGS : **Are Bookings Necessary :** Yes   **CONTACT NUMBER :** (0706) 44648

ROTHERHAM UNITED FC

WHEELCHAIRS : **Location of Accommodation :** Accommodated in Disabled Section - Millmoor Lane
Nº Spaces for Home Fans; Nº Spaces for Away Fans : 7 spaces available
Are Helpers Admitted; Nº Admitted : One helper admitted per disabled person
PRICES : **Prices for Disabled; Prices for Helpers :** Free of charge for both the disabled and helpers
TOILETS : **Location of Disabled Toilets (+ Number) :** None
BLIND : **Facilities Available :** No Special Facilities
BOOKINGS : **Are Bookings Necessary :** Yes   **CONTACT NUMBER :** (0709) 562434

SCARBOROUGH FC

WHEELCHAIRS : **Location of Accommodation :** Adjacent to Main Stand
Nº Spaces for Home Fans; Nº Spaces for Away Fans : 3 spaces available in total
Are Helpers Admitted; Nº Admitted : One helper admitted per wheelchair
PRICES : **Prices for Disabled; Prices for Helpers :** Full-price for both the disabled and helpers
TOILETS : **Location of Disabled Toilets (+ Number) :** None
BLIND : **Facilities Available :** No Special Facilities
BOOKINGS : **Are Bookings Necessary :** Yes   **CONTACT NUMBER :** (0723) 375094

SCUNTHORPE UNITED FC

WHEELCHAIRS : **Location of Accommodation :** Accommodated in Disabled Section - Clugston Stand
Nº Spaces for Home Fans; Nº Spaces for Away Fans : 12 spaces each for home & away fans
Are Helpers Admitted; Nº Admitted : One helper admitted per disabled fan
PRICES : **Prices for Disabled; Prices for Helpers :** Free of charge for the disabled. Full-price for helpers
TOILETS : **Location of Disabled Toilets (+ Number) :** One in the Clugston Stand
BLIND : **Facilities Available :** Commentaries Available
BOOKINGS : **Are Bookings Necessary :** Yes   **CONTACT NUMBER :** (0724) 848077

SHEFFIELD UNITED FC

WHEELCHAIRS : **Location of Accommodation :** Accommodated in Disabled Section - Members Area
Nº Spaces for Home Fans; Nº Spaces for Away Fans : Limited for number available
Are Helpers Admitted; Nº Admitted : One helper admitted per wheelchair
PRICES : **Prices for Disabled; Prices for Helpers :** Free of charge for both the disabled and helpers
TOILETS : **Location of Disabled Toilets (+ Number) :** 3 available within the enclosure
BLIND : **Facilities Available :** Commentaries Available on Request
BOOKINGS : **Are Bookings Necessary :** Yes   **CONTACT NUMBER :** (0742) 738955

SHEFFIELD WEDNESDAY FC

WHEELCHAIRS : **Location of Accommodation :** Accommodated in Disabled Section - North Stand
Nº Spaces for Home Fans; Nº Spaces for Away Fans : Number not specified
Are Helpers Admitted; Nº Admitted : One helper admitted per disabled supporter
PRICES : **Prices for Disabled; Prices for Helpers :** Normal Prices for both the disabled and helpers
TOILETS : **Location of Disabled Toilets (+ Number) :** Available within the North Stand
BLIND : **Facilities Available :** Commentaries Available
BOOKINGS : **Are Bookings Necessary :** Yes   **CONTACT NUMBER :** (0742) 343122

SHREWSBURY TOWN FC

WHEELCHAIRS :	**Location of Accommodation**: No specific area, but along pitchside if necessary
	Nº Spaces for Home Fans; Nº Spaces for Away Fans: No fixed numbers
	Are Helpers Admitted; Nº Admitted: One helper per disabled supporter
PRICES :	**Prices for Disabled; Prices for Helpers**: Free of charge for the disabled. Full-price for helpers
TOILETS :	**Location of Disabled Toilets (+ Number)**: None
BLIND :	**Facilities Available**: No Special Facilities but can be accommodated
BOOKINGS :	**Are Bookings Necessary**: Yes **CONTACT NUMBER**: (0743) 360111

SOUTHAMPTON FC

WHEELCHAIRS :	**Location of Accommodation**: Limited Accommodation - Under West Stand
	Nº Spaces for Home Fans; Nº Spaces for Away Fans: 12 spaces available in total
	Are Helpers Admitted; Nº Admitted: One helper admitted per disabled person
PRICES :	**Prices for Disabled; Prices for Helpers**: Free of charge for the disabled. Helpers £8.00/£10.00
TOILETS :	**Location of Disabled Toilets (+ Number)**: By disabled entrance
BLIND :	**Facilities Available**: Commentaries Available
BOOKINGS :	**Are Bookings Necessary**: Yes **CONTACT NUMBER**: (0489) 784515 Mr.Mortimer

SOUTHEND UNITED FC

WHEELCHAIRS :	**Location of Accommodation**: Accommodated in Disabled Section - West Stand
	Nº Spaces for Home Fans; Nº Spaces for Away Fans: 20 spaces available in total
	Are Helpers Admitted; Nº Admitted: One helper admitted per disabled person
PRICES :	**Prices for Disabled; Prices for Helpers**: £4.00 per wheelchair. £8 per helper (1991/92 prices)
TOILETS :	**Location of Disabled Toilets (+ Number)**: One available in disabled area
BLIND :	**Facilities Available**: Commentaries Available
BOOKINGS :	**Are Bookings Necessary**: Yes **CONTACT NUMBER**: (0702) 435602

STOCKPORT COUNTY FC

WHEELCHAIRS :	**Location of Accommodation**: Accommodated in Disabled Section
	Nº Spaces for Home Fans; Nº Spaces for Away Fans: Spaces available for 10 wheelchairs
	Are Helpers Admitted; Nº Admitted: One helper admitted per disabled supporter
PRICES :	**Prices for Disabled; Prices for Helpers**: Free of charge for the disabled. Full-price for helpers
TOILETS :	**Location of Disabled Toilets (+ Number)**: None
BLIND :	**Facilities Available**: None
BOOKINGS :	**Are Bookings Necessary**: Yes **CONTACT NUMBER**: (061) 480-8888

STOKE CITY FC

WHEELCHAIRS :	**Location of Accommodation**: In Disabled Section - Corner Butler Street/Boothen End
	Nº Spaces for Home Fans; Nº Spaces for Away Fans: 25 spaces available in total
	Are Helpers Admitted; Nº Admitted: One helper admitted per disabled person
PRICES :	**Prices for Disabled; Prices for Helpers**: Free of charge for both the disabled and helpers
TOILETS :	**Location of Disabled Toilets (+ Number)**: None
BLIND :	**Facilities Available**: Limited Facilities - Phone First
BOOKINGS :	**Are Bookings Necessary**: Yes **CONTACT NUMBER**: (0782) 413511

SUNDERLAND AFC

WHEELCHAIRS :	**Location of Accommodation**: Accommodated in Disabled Section - Roker End
	Nº Spaces for Home Fans; Nº Spaces for Away Fans: 21 spaces for home fans; 22 for away
	Are Helpers Admitted; Nº Admitted: One helper admitted per disabled person
PRICES :	**Prices for Disabled; Prices for Helpers**: Free of charge for both the disabled and helpers
TOILETS :	**Location of Disabled Toilets (+ Number)**: Toilets available in Roker End & Fulwell End
BLIND :	**Facilities Available**: Headphone Commentaries Available in Disabled Section (Main Stand)
BOOKINGS :	**Are Bookings Necessary**: Yes **CONTACT NUMBER**: (091) 514-0332

SWANSEA CITY FC

WHEELCHAIRS :	**Location of Accommodation**: Accommodated - Centre Stand Touchline
	Nº Spaces for Home Fans; Nº Spaces for Away Fans: Approximately 10 spaces available
	Are Helpers Admitted; Nº Admitted: One helper admitted per wheelchair
PRICES :	**Prices for Disabled; Prices for Helpers**: Free of Charge for both the disabled and helpers
TOILETS :	**Location of Disabled Toilets (+ Number)**: None
BLIND :	**Facilities Available**: No Special Facilities
BOOKINGS :	**Are Bookings Necessary**: Yes **CONTACT NUMBER**: (0792) 474114

SWINDON TOWN FC

WHEELCHAIRS :	**Location of Accommodation**: Accommodated in Disabled Section - North Stand
	Nº Spaces for Home Fans; Nº Spaces for Away Fans: 40 spaces available in total
	Are Helpers Admitted; Nº Admitted: One helper admitted per disabled supporter
PRICES :	**Prices for Disabled; Prices for Helpers**: Free of charge for both the disabled and helpers
TOILETS :	**Location of Disabled Toilets (+ Number)**: One available within the Enclosure
BLIND :	**Facilities Available**: Commentaries Available in Disabled Section
BOOKINGS :	**Are Bookings Necessary**: Yes **CONTACT NUMBER**: (0793) 430430

TORQUAY UNITED FC

WHEELCHAIRS :	**Location of Accommodation**: Accommodated in the Main Stand
	Nº Spaces for Home Fans; Nº Spaces for Away Fans: Not Specified
	Are Helpers Admitted; Nº Admitted: One helper admitted per disabled supporter
PRICES :	**Prices for Disabled; Prices for Helpers**: Free of charge for both the disabled and helpers
TOILETS :	**Location of Disabled Toilets (+ Number)**: 2 toilets available in Main Stand
BLIND :	**Facilities Available**: Audio Facilities Available
BOOKINGS :	**Are Bookings Necessary**: Yes **CONTACT NUMBER**: (0803) 328666

TOTTENHAM HOTSPUR FC

WHEELCHAIRS :	**Location of Accommodation**: Accommodated - Paxton Road End & West Stand Lower Tier
	Nº Spaces for Home Fans; Nº Spaces for Away Fans: 45 spaces available in total
	Are Helpers Admitted; Nº Admitted: One helper admitted per disabled person
PRICES :	**Prices for Disabled; Prices for Helpers**: Free of charge for the disabled. Helpers £10.00
TOILETS :	**Location of Disabled Toilets (+ Number)**: One available in West Stand Lower Tier
BLIND :	**Facilities Available**: No Special Facilities
BOOKINGS :	**Are Bookings Necessary**: Yes **CONTACT NUMBER**: (081) 808-8080 ext. 271

TRANMERE ROVERS FC

WHEELCHAIRS :	**Location of Accommodation**: Accommodated in Disabled Section - Family Enclosure
	Nº Spaces for Home Fans; Nº Spaces for Away Fans: 25 spaces available in total
	Are Helpers Admitted; Nº Admitted: One helper admitted per disabled supporter
PRICES :	**Prices for Disabled; Prices for Helpers**: Free of charge for the disabled. Helpers £6.00
TOILETS :	**Location of Disabled Toilets (+ Number)**: In Disabled Section - 2 available
BLIND :	**Facilities Available**: No Special Facilities
BOOKINGS :	**Are Bookings Necessary**: Yes **CONTACT NUMBER**: (051) 608-0371

WALSALL FC

WHEELCHAIRS :	**Location of Accommodation**: Accommodated in Highgate Mild Stand
	Nº Spaces for Home Fans; Nº Spaces for Away Fans: Total of 30 spaces available
	Are Helpers Admitted; Nº Admitted: One adult helper admitted per disabled person
PRICES :	**Prices for Disabled; Prices for Helpers**: Free of charge for both the disabled and helpers
TOILETS :	**Location of Disabled Toilets (+ Number)**: Adjacent to disabled viewing bays
BLIND :	**Facilities Available**: Commentaries Planned
BOOKINGS :	**Are Bookings Necessary**: Yes **CONTACT NUMBER**: (0922) 22791

WATFORD FC

WHEELCHAIRS :	**Location of Accommodation**: Accommodated in Disabled Section - East Stand
	Nº Spaces for Home Fans; Nº Spaces for Away Fans: Approximately 25 spaces in total
	Are Helpers Admitted; Nº Admitted: One helper admitted per disabled person
PRICES :	**Prices for Disabled; Prices for Helpers**: £5.00 Adult, £3.00 Child for both disabled and helpers
TOILETS :	**Location of Disabled Toilets (+ Number)**: Adjacent to Enclosure
BLIND :	**Facilities Available**: Commentaries Available in Disabled Section
BOOKINGS :	**Are Bookings Necessary**: No **CONTACT NUMBER**: (0923) 220393

WEST BROMWICH ALBION FC

WHEELCHAIRS :	**Location of Accommodation**: Accommodated - Corner Birmingham Road End/Main Stand
	Nº Spaces for Home Fans; Nº Spaces for Away Fans: 30 spaces in total
	Are Helpers Admitted; Nº Admitted: One helper admitted per disabled person
PRICES :	**Prices for Disabled; Prices for Helpers**: Free of charge for both the disabled and helpers
TOILETS :	**Location of Disabled Toilets (+ Number)**: One available within the disabled section
BLIND :	**Facilities Available**: Accommodation for six listeners and six guides
BOOKINGS :	**Are Bookings Necessary**: Yes **CONTACT NUMBER**: (021) 525-8888

WEST HAM UNITED FC

WHEELCHAIRS :   **Location of Accommodation**: Limited Accommodation in Disabled Area - West Stand
N⁰ Spaces for Home Fans; N⁰ Spaces for Away Fans: 16 spaces for home fans, 4 for away
Are Helpers Admitted; N⁰ Admitted: Yes
PRICES :   **Prices for Disabled; Prices for Helpers**: Free of charge for the disabled. Helpers £5.00
TOILETS :   **Location of Disabled Toilets (+ Number)**: One available 200 yards from the Disabled Area
BLIND :   **Facilities Available**: No Special Facilities
BOOKINGS :   **Are Bookings Necessary**: Yes   **CONTACT NUMBER**: (081) 472-2740

WIGAN ATHLETIC FC

WHEELCHAIRS :   **Location of Accommodation**: Accommodated - Disabled Unit within Jewsons Enclosure
N⁰ Spaces for Home Fans; N⁰ Spaces for Away Fans: 10 spaces in total
Are Helpers Admitted; N⁰ Admitted: One helper admitted per disabled person
PRICES :   **Prices for Disabled; Prices for Helpers**: Free of charge for the disabled. Helpers £4.50
TOILETS :   **Location of Disabled Toilets (+ Number)**: None
BLIND :   **Facilities Available**: Commentaries Available in Phoenix Stand
BOOKINGS :   **Are Bookings Necessary**: Yes   **CONTACT NUMBER**: (0942) 44433

WIMBLEDON FC

WHEELCHAIRS :   **Location of Accommodation**: In Disabled Section - Arthur Wait Stand (Park Road Entrance)
N⁰ Spaces for Home Fans; N⁰ Spaces for Away Fans: 25 spaces for Home fans; 4 for Away
Are Helpers Admitted; N⁰ Admitted: One helper admitted per disabled supporter
PRICES :   **Prices for Disabled; Prices for Helpers**: Disabled Free of charge. Helpers charged full-price
TOILETS :   **Location of Disabled Toilets (+ Number)**: Located in Disabled Section
BLIND :   **Facilities Available**: Commentaries Available - 4 places
BOOKINGS :   **Are Bookings Necessary**: Yes   **CONTACT NUMBER**: (081) 771-8841

WOLVERHAMPTON WANDERERS FC

WHEELCHAIRS :   **Location of Accommodation**: Accommodated in Disabled Section - Stan Cullis Stand
N⁰ Spaces for Home Fans; N⁰ Spaces for Away Fans: 50 spaces available in total
Are Helpers Admitted; N⁰ Admitted: One helper admitted per wheelchair
PRICES :   **Prices for Disabled; Prices for Helpers**: Free of charge for the disabled. £6.00 for helpers
TOILETS :   **Location of Disabled Toilets (+ Number)**: Toilets at both ends of Stan Cullis Stand
BLIND :   **Facilities Available**: No Special Facilities
BOOKINGS :   **Are Bookings Necessary**: No   **CONTACT NUMBER**: (0902) 25899

WREXHAM FC

WHEELCHAIRS :   **Location of Accommodation**: Accommodated in Disabled Section - Mold Road Side
N⁰ Spaces for Home Fans; N⁰ Spaces for Away Fans: 18 spaces in total
Are Helpers Admitted; N⁰ Admitted: One helper admitted per wheelchair
PRICES :   **Prices for Disabled; Prices for Helpers**: Free of charge for the disabled. £4.00 per helper
TOILETS :   **Location of Disabled Toilets (+ Number)**: None
BLIND :   **Facilities Available**: Commentaries Available (By Hospital Radio Broadcasters)
BOOKINGS :   **Are Bookings Necessary**: Yes   **CONTACT NUMBER**: (0978) 351332

YORK CITY FC

WHEELCHAIRS :   **Location of Accommodation**: Accommodated in Disabled Section - In front of Enclosure
N⁰ Spaces for Home Fans; N⁰ Spaces for Away Fans: 6 spaces available for home fans only
Are Helpers Admitted; N⁰ Admitted: One helper admitted per disabled person
PRICES :   **Prices for Disabled; Prices for Helpers**: Free of charge for the disabled. Helpers £5.00
TOILETS :   **Location of Disabled Toilets (+ Number)**: None at present   (See Note on Club page)
BLIND :   **Facilities Available**: Commentaries Available
BOOKINGS :   **Are Bookings Necessary**: No   **CONTACT NUMBER**: (0904) 624447

1st Division Season 1991/92	ARSENAL	LIVERPOOL	C. PALACE	LEEDS UTD	MAN. CITY	MAN. UTD	WIMBLEDON	NOTTS. FOR.	EVERTON	SPURS	CHELSEA	QPR	SHEFF. UTD	SOTON	NORWICH	COVENTRY	ASTON VILLA	LUTON TOWN	OLDHAM ATH.	W. HAM UTD	SHEFF. WED.	NOTTS. CO.
ARSENAL		4-0	4-1	1-1	2-1	1-1	1-1	3-3	4-2	2-0	3-2	1-1	5-2	5-1	1-1	1-2	0-0	2-0	2-1	0-1	7-1	2-0
LIVERPOOL	2-0		1-2	0-0	2-2	2-0	2-3	2-0	3-1	2-1	1-2	1-0	2-1	0-0	2-1	1-0	1-1	2-1	2-1	1-0	1-1	4-0
CRYST. PALACE	1-4	1-0		1-0	1-1	1-3	3-2	0-0	2-0	1-2	0-0	2-2	2-1	1-0	3-4	0-1	0-0	1-1	0-0	2-3	1-1	1-0
LEEDS UTD	2-2	1-0	1-1		3-0	1-1	5-1	1-0	1-0	1-1	3-0	2-0	4-3	3-3	1-0	2-0	0-0	2-0	1-0	0-0	1-1	3-0
MAN. CITY	1-0	2-1	3-2	4-0		0-0	0-0	2-1	0-1	1-0	0-0	2-2	3-2	0-1	2-1	1-0	2-0	4-0	1-2	2-0	0-1	2-0
MAN. UTD	1-1	0-0	2-0	1-1	1-1		0-0	1-2	1-0	3-1	1-1	1-4	2-0	1-0	3-0	4-0	1-0	5-0	1-0	2-1	1-1	2-0
WIMBLEDON	1-3	0-0	1-1	0-0	2-1	1-2		3-0	0-0	3-5	1-2	0-1	3-0	0-1	3-1	1-1	2-0	3-0	2-1	2-0	2-1	2-0
NOTTS. FOREST	3-2	1-1	5-1	0-0	2-0	1-0	4-2		2-1	1-3	1-1	1-1	2-5	1-3	2-0	1-0	2-0	1-1	3-1	2-2	0-2	1-1
EVERTON	3-1	1-1	2-2	1-1	1-2	0-0	2-0	1-1		3-1	2-1	0-0	0-2	0-1	1-1	3-0	0-2	1-1	1-1	4-0	0-1	1-0
TOTT. HOTSPUR	1-1	1-2	0-1	1-3	0-1	1-2	3-2	1-2	3-3		1-3	2-0	0-1	1-2	3-0	4-3	2-5	4-1	0-0	3-0	0-2	2-1
CHELSEA	1-1	2-2	1-1	0-1	1-1	1-3	2-2	1-0	2-2	2-0		2-1	1-2	1-1	0-3	0-1	2-0	4-1	4-2	2-1	0-3	2-2
Q. PK. RANGERS	0-0	0-0	1-0	4-1	4-0	0-0	1-1	0-2	3-1	1-2	2-2		1-0	2-2	0-2	1-1	0-1	2-1	1-3	0-0	1-1	1-1
SHEFF. UTD	1-1	2-0	1-1	2-3	4-2	1-2	0-0	4-2	2-1	2-0	0-1	0-0		0-2	1-0	0-3	2-0	1-1	2-0	1-1	2-0	1-3
SOUTHAMPTON	0-4	1-1	1-0	0-4	0-3	0-1	1-0	0-1	1-2	2-3	1-0	2-1	2-4		0-0	0-0	1-1	2-1	1-0	1-0	0-1	1-1
NORWICH CITY	1-3	3-0	3-3	2-2	0-0	1-3	1-1	0-0	4-3	0-1	0-1	0-1	2-2	2-1		3-2	2-1	1-0	1-2	2-1	1-0	0-1
COVENTRY CITY	0-1	0-0	1-2	0-0	0-1	0-0	0-1	0-2	0-1	1-2	0-1	2-2	3-1	2-0	0-0		1-0	5-0	1-1	0-0	0-0	1-0
ASTON VILLA	3-1	1-0	0-1	1-4	3-1	0-1	2-1	3-1	0-0	0-0	3-1	0-1	1-1	2-1	1-0	2-0		4-0	1-0	3-1	0-1	1-0
LUTON TOWN	1-0	0-0	1-1	0-2	2-2	1-1	2-1	2-1	0-1	0-0	2-0	1-0	2-1	2-1	2-0	1-0	2-0		2-1	0-1	2-2	1-1
OLDHAM ATH.	1-1	2-3	2-3	2-0	2-5	3-6	0-1	2-1	2-2	1-0	3-0	2-1	2-1	1-1	2-2	2-1	3-2	5-1		2-2	3-0	4-3
WEST HAM UTD	0-2	0-0	0-2	1-3	1-2	1-0	1-1	3-0	0-2	2-1	1-1	2-2	1-1	0-1	4-0	0-1	3-1	0-0	1-0		1-2	0-2
SHEFF. WED.	1-1	0-0	4-1	1-6	2-0	3-2	2-0	2-1	2-1	0-0	3-0	4-1	1-3	2-0	2-0	1-1	2-3	3-2	1-1	2-1		1-0
NOTTS COUNTY	0-1	1-2	2-3	2-4	1-3	1-1	1-1	0-4	0-0	0-2	2-0	0-1	1-3	1-0	2-2	1-0	0-0	2-1	2-0	3-0	2-1	

Team	P	W	D	L	F	A	Pts
Leeds United	42	22	16	4	74	37	82
Manchester Utd	42	21	15	6	63	33	78
Sheff. Wednes.	42	21	12	9	62	49	75
Arsenal	42	19	15	8	81	46	72
Manchester City	42	20	10	12	61	48	70
Liverpool	42	16	16	10	47	40	64
Aston Villa	42	17	9	16	48	44	60
Nottingham For.	42	16	11	15	60	58	59
Sheffield United	42	16	9	17	65	63	57
Crystal Palace	42	14	15	13	53	61	57
Queens Pk Rgrs	42	12	18	12	48	47	54
Everton	42	13	14	15	52	51	53
Wimbledon	42	13	14	15	53	53	53
Chelsea	42	13	14	15	50	60	53
Tott. Hotspur	42	15	7	20	58	63	52
Southampton	42	14	10	18	39	55	52
Oldham Athletic	42	14	9	19	63	67	51
Norwich City	42	11	12	19	47	63	45
Coventry City	42	11	11	20	35	44	44
Luton Town	42	10	12	20	38	71	42
Notts County	42	10	10	22	40	62	40
West Ham Utd	42	9	11	22	37	59	38

Champions : - Leeds United

Relegated : - Luton Town, Notts County & West Ham United

All statistics provided by David Clayton & Jan Buitenga from their new book 'FOOTBALL IN EUROPE 1991/92' which can be obtained via the Soccer Bookshelf - priced £11.95 per copy + £1.25 postage.

2nd Division — Season 1991/92

	SUND'LAND	DERBY CO.	MILLWALL	BRIGHTON	MIDDLESBR'	BARNSLEY	BRISTOL C.	OXFORD U.	NEWCASTLE	WOLVES	BRISTOL R.	IPSWICH T.	PORT VALE	CHARLTON	PORTSM'TH	PLYMOUTH	BLACKBURN	WATFORD	SWINDON	LEICESTER	CAMBRIDGE	SOUTHEND	GRIMSBY T.	TRANMERE
SUNDERLAND	■	1-1	6-2	4-2	2-0	1-3	2-0	1-1	1-0	1-1	3-0	1-1	1-2	1-0	0-1	1-1	3-1	0-0	1-0	2-2	1-2	1-2	1-2	1-1
DERBY CNTY.	1-2	■	0-2	3-1	2-0	1-1	4-1	2-2	4-1	1-2	1-0	1-0	3-1	1-2	2-0	2-0	0-2	3-1	2-1	1-2	0-0	1-2	0-0	0-1
MILLWALL	4-1	1-2	■	1-2	2-0	1-1	2-3	2-1	2-1	2-1	0-1	2-3	1-0	1-0	1-1	2-1	1-3	0-4	1-1	2-0	1-2	2-0	1-1	0-3
BRIGHTON	2-2	1-2	3-4	■	1-1	3-1	0-0	1-2	2-2	3-3	3-1	2-2	3-1	1-2	2-1	1-0	0-3	0-1	0-2	1-2	1-1	3-2	3-0	0-2
MIDDLESBR.	2-1	1-1	1-0	4-0	■	0-1	3-1	2-1	3-0	0-0	2-1	1-1	2-0	2-0	2-1	0-0	1-2	2-2	3-0	1-1	1-1	2-0	1-0	
BARNSLEY	0-3	0-3	0-2	1-2	2-1	■	1-2	1-0	3-0	2-0	0-1	1-0	0-0	1-1	0-3	2-1	0-3	1-1	3-1	0-0	1-0	4-1	1-1	
BRISTOL CITY	1-0	1-2	2-2	2-1	1-1	0-2	■	1-1	1-1	2-0	1-0	2-1	3-0	0-2	0-2	2-0	1-0	1-0	1-1	2-1	1-2	2-2	1-1	2-2
OXFORD U.	3-0	2-0	2-2	3-1	1-2	0-1	1-1	■	5-2	1-0	2-2	1-1	2-2	1-2	2-1	3-2	1-3	0-0	5-3	1-2	1-0	0-1	1-2	1-0
NEWCASTLE U.	1-0	2-2	0-1	0-1	0-1	1-1	3-0	4-3	■	1-2	2-1	1-1	2-2	3-4	1-0	2-2	0-0	2-2	3-1	2-0	1-1	3-2	2-0	2-3
WOLVES	1-0	2-3	0-0	2-0	1-2	1-2	1-1	3-1	6-2	■	2-3	1-2	0-2	1-1	0-0	1-0	0-0	3-0	2-1	1-0	2-1	3-1	1-1	1-1
BRISTOL RVRS	2-1	2-3	3-2	4-1	2-1	0-0	3-2	2-1	1-2	1-1	■	3-3	3-3	1-0	1-0	0-0	3-0	1-1	1-1	1-1	2-2	4-1	2-3	1-0
IPSWICH T.	0-1	2-1	0-0	3-1	2-1	2-0	4-2	2-1	3-2	2-1	1-0	■	2-1	2-0	5-2	2-0	2-1	1-2	1-4	0-0	1-2	1-0	0-0	4-0
PORT VALE	3-3	1-0	0-2	2-1	1-2	1-2	2-1	2-1	0-1	1-1	0-1	1-2	■	1-1	1-0	2-0	2-1	2-2	1-2	1-0	0-0	0-1	1-1	
CHARLT. A.	1-4	0-2	1-0	2-0	0-0	1-1	2-1	2-2	2-1	0-2	1-0	1-1	2-0	■	3-0	0-0	0-2	1-1	0-0	2-0	1-2	2-0	1-3	0-1
PORTSMTH.	1-0	0-1	6-1	0-0	4-0	2-0	1-0	2-1	3-1	1-0	2-0	1-1	1-0	1-2	■	4-1	2-2	0-0	1-1	1-0	3-0	1-1	2-0	2-0
PLYM. ARG.	1-0	1-1	3-2	1-1	1-1	2-1	1-0	3-1	2-0	1-0	1-0	1-0	0-2	3-2	■	1-3	0-1	0-4	2-2	0-1	0-2	1-2	1-0	
BLACK. RVRS	2-2	2-0	2-1	1-0	2-1	3-0	4-0	1-1	3-1	1-2	3-0	1-2	0-2	1-1	5-2		■	1-0	2-1	0-1	2-1	2-2	2-1	0-0
WATFORD	1-0	1-2	0-2	0-1	1-2	1-1	5-2	2-0	2-2	0-2	1-0	0-1	0-0	2-0	2-1	1-0	2-1	■	0-0	0-1	1-3	1-2	2-0	1-0
SWINDON T.	5-3	1-2	3-1	2-1	0-1	3-1	2-0	2-1	2-1	1-2	1-0	1-0	0-0	1-2	2-3	1-0	2-1	3-1	■	0-0	2-0	3-1	1-1	2-0
LEICESTER C.	3-2	1-1	1-1	4-1	2-1	2-1	2-1	1-2	3-0	1-1	2-2	2-0	0-2	0-2	2-0	3-0	1-2	3-1		■	2-1	2-0	2-0	1-0
CAMBRIDGE U.	3-0	0-0	1-0	0-0	0-0	2-1	0-0	1-1	0-2	2-1	6-1	1-1	4-2	1-0	2-2	1-1	2-1	0-1	3-2	5-1	■	0-1	0-1	0-0
SOUTHEND U.	2-0	1-0	2-3	2-1	0-1	2-1	1-1	2-3	4-0	0-2	2-0	2-1	0-0	1-1	2-3	2-1	3-0	1-0	3-2	1-2	1-1	■	3-1	1-1
GRIMSBY T.	2-0	0-1	1-1	0-1	1-0	0-1	3-1	1-0	1-1	0-2	0-1	1-2	1-2	1-0	1-1	2-3	0-1	0-0	0-1	3-4	3-2		■	2-2
TRANM. RVRS	1-0	4-3	2-1	1-1	1-2	2-1	2-2	1-2	3-2	4-3	2-2	0-1	2-1	2-2	2-0	1-0	2-2	1-1	0-0	1-2	1-2	1-1	1-1	■

	P	W	D	L	F	A	Pts
Ipswich Town	46	24	12	10	70	50	84
Middlesbrough	46	23	11	12	58	41	80
Derby County	46	23	9	14	69	51	78
Leicester City	46	23	8	15	62	55	77
Cambridge Utd	46	19	17	10	65	47	74
Blackburn Rvrs	46	21	11	14	70	53	74
Charlton Athletic	46	20	11	15	54	48	71
Swindon Town	46	18	15	13	69	55	69
Portsmouth	46	19	12	15	65	51	69
Watford	46	18	11	17	51	48	65
Wolver. Wands.	46	18	10	18	61	54	64
Southend United	46	17	11	18	63	63	62
Bristol Rovers	46	16	14	16	60	63	62
Tranmere Rvrs	46	14	19	13	56	56	61
Millwall	46	17	10	19	64	71	61
Barnsley	46	16	11	19	46	57	59
Bristol City	46	13	15	18	55	71	54
Sunderland	46	14	11	21	61	65	53
Grimsby Town	46	14	11	21	47	62	53
Newcastle Utd	46	13	13	20	66	84	52
Oxford United	46	13	11	22	66	73	50
Plymouth Argyle	46	13	9	24	42	64	48
Brighton & Hove	46	12	11	23	56	77	47
Port Vale	46	10	15	21	42	59	45

PROMOTION PLAY-OFFS

Blackburn Rovers 4   Derby County 2
Cambridge United 1   Leicester City 1

Derby County 2   Blackburn Rovers 1
Blackburn Rovers win 5-4 on aggregate
Leicester City 5   Cambridge United 0
Leicester City win 6-1 on aggregate

Blackburn Rovers 1   Leicester City 0

Promoted : - Ipswich Town, Middlesbrough & Blackburn Rovers

Relegated : - Plymouth Argyle, Brighton & Hove Albion & Port Vale

3rd Division — Season 1991/92

	WEST BR.	HULL CITY	BOLTON W.	BRENTF'D	BURY	BRADFORD	BOURNE'TH	WIGAN ATH.	HUDDERSF.	BIRM'HAM	LEYTON OR.	STOKE CITY	READING	EXETER C.	PRESTON	SHREWSB.	CHESTER	SWANSEA	FULHAM	DARLINGT.	STOCKP'T	HARTPOOL	PETERBRO'	TORQUAY U.
WEST BROM.	■	1-0	2-2	2-0	1-1	1-1	4-0	1-1	2-1	0-1	1-3	2-2	2-0	6-3	3-0	2-0	1-1	2-3	2-3	3-1	1-0	1-2	4-0	1-0
HULL CITY	1-0	■	2-0	0-3	0-1	0-0	0-1	1-1	1-0	1-2	1-0	0-1	0-1	1-2	2-2	4-0	1-0	3-0	0-0	5-2	0-2	0-2	1-2	4-1
BOLTON WANDS.	3-0	1-0	■	1-2	2-1	1-1	0-2	1-1	1-1	1-1	1-0	3-1	1-1	1-2	1-0	1-0	0-0	0-0	0-3	2-0	0-0	2-2	2-1	1-0
BRENTFORD	1-2	4-1	3-2	■	0-3	3-4	2-2	4-0	2-3	2-2	4-3	2-0	1-0	3-0	1-0	2-0	2-0	3-2	4-0	4-1	2-1	1-0	2-1	3-2
BURY	1-1	3-2	1-1	0-3	■	0-1	0-1	1-4	4-4	1-0	4-2	1-3	0-1	3-1	2-3	0-0	1-2	1-0	3-1	1-0	0-0	1-1	3-0	0-0
BRADFORD C.	1-1	2-1	4-4	0-1	1-1	■	3-1	1-1	1-1	1-2	1-1	1-0	1-0	1-1	1-1	3-0	1-1	4-6	3-4	0-1	1-0	1-1	2-1	2-0
BOURNEMOUTH	2-1	0-0	1-2	0-0	4-0	1-3	■	3-0	1-1	2-1	0-1	1-2	3-2	1-0	1-0	1-0	2-0	3-0	0-0	1-2	1-0	2-0	1-2	2-1
WIGAN ATH.	0-1	0-1	1-1	2-1	2-0	2-1	2-0	■	1-3	3-0	1-1	3-0	1-1	4-1	3-0	1-1	2-1	1-0	0-2	1-2	1-3	1-1	3-0	1-0
HUDDERS. T.	3-0	1-1	1-0	2-1	3-0	1-0	0-0	3-1	■	3-2	1-0	1-2	1-2	0-0	1-2	2-1	1-0	3-1	2-1	0-1	1-0	0-0		4-0
BIRMINGHAM C.	0-3	2-2	2-1	1-0	3-2	2-0	0-1	3-3	2-0	■	2-2	1-1	2-0	1-0	3-1	1-0	3-2	1-1	3-1	1-0	3-0	2-1	1-1	3-0
LEYTON O.	1-1	1-0	2-1	4-2	4-0	1-1	1-1	3-1	1-0	0-0	■	0-1	1-1	0-0	2-0	1-0	1-0	1-2	2-2	3-0	3-3	4-0	1-2	3-2
STOKE C.	1-0	2-3	2-0	2-1	1-2	0-0	1-1	3-0	0-2	2-1	2-0	■	3-0	5-2	2-1	1-0	0-1	2-1	2-2	3-0	2-2	3-2	3-3	
READING	1-2	0-1	1-0	0-0	3-2	1-2	0-0	3-2	1-0	1-1	3-2	3-4	■	1-0	2-2	2-1	0-0	1-0	0-2	2-2	1-1	0-1	1-1	6-1
EXETER C.	1-1	0-3	2-2	1-2	5-2	1-0	0-3	0-1	0-1	2-1	2-0	0-0	2-1	■	4-1	1-0	1-0	2-1	1-1	4-1	2-1	1-1	2-2	1-0
PRESTON N.E.	2-0	3-1	2-1	1-3	2-0	1-1	2-2	2-3	1-0	3-2	2-1	2-2	1-1	1-3	■	2-2	0-3	1-1	1-2	3-2	1-4	1-1	1-3	3-0
SHREWS. T.	1-3	2-3	1-3	1-0	1-1	3-2	1-2	1-0	1-1	1-1	0-1	1-0	1-2	6-1	2-0	■	2-2	0-0	0-0	0-2	0-1	1-4	2-0	2-2
CHESTER C.	1-2	1-1	0-1	1-1	3-1	0-0	0-1	1-0	0-0	0-1	1-0	0-0	2-2	5-2	3-2	1-4	■	2-0	2-0	2-5	3-2	2-0	2-4	2-0
SWANSEA C.	0-0	0-0	1-1	1-1	2-1	2-2	3-1	3-0	0-1	0-2	2-2	2-1	1-2	0-0	2-2	1-2	3-0	■	2-2	4-2	2-1	1-1	1-0	1-0
FULHAM	0-0	0-0	1-1	0-1	4-2	2-1	2-0	1-1	1-0	0-1	2-1	1-1	1-0	0-0	1-0	0-1	2-2	3-0	■	4-0	1-2	1-0	0-1	2-1
STOCKPORT CO.	3-0	1-1	2-2	2-1	2-0	4-1	5-0	3-3	0-0	2-0	1-0	0-0	1-0	4-1	2-0	1-4	0-4	5-0	2-0		■	0-1	3-0	2-1
HARTLEPOOL U.	0-0	2-3	0-4	1-0	0-0	1-0	1-0	4-3	0-0	1-0	0-0	2-3	1-0	2-0	3-1	2-0	4-2	1-0	0-1	2-0	0-1	■	0-1	1-1
PETERBR. U.	0-0	3-0	1-0	0-1	0-0	2-1	2-0	0-0	2-0	2-3	0-2	1-1	5-3	1-1	1-0	1-0	2-0	3-1	4-1	1-1	3-2	3-2	■	1-1
TORQUAY U.	1-0	2-1	2-0	1-1	0-2	1-1	1-0	0-1	0-1	1-2	1-0	1-0	1-2	1-0	1-0	1-2	3-2	1-0	0-1	3-0	2-0	3-1	2-2	■

Team	P	W	D	L	F	A	Pts
Brentford	46	25	7	14	81	55	82
Birmingham City	46	23	12	11	69	52	81
Huddersfield Tn.	46	22	12	12	59	38	78
Stoke City	46	21	14	11	69	49	77
Stockport Co.	46	22	10	14	75	51	76
Peterboro' Utd	46	20	14	12	65	58	74
West Brom. Alb.	46	19	14	13	64	49	71
Bournemouth	46	20	11	15	52	48	71
Fulham	46	19	13	14	57	53	70
Leyton Orient	46	18	11	17	62	52	65
Hartlepool Utd	46	18	11	17	57	57	65
Reading	46	16	13	17	59	62	61
Bolton Wands.	46	14	17	15	57	56	59
Hull City	46	16	11	19	54	54	59
Wigan Athletic	46	15	14	17	58	64	59
Bradford City	46	13	19	14	62	61	58
Preston N'th End	46	15	12	19	61	72	57
Chester City	46	14	14	18	56	59	56
Swansea City	46	14	14	18	55	65	56
Exeter City	46	14	11	21	57	80	53
Bury	46	13	12	21	55	74	51
Shrewsbury Tn.	46	12	11	23	53	68	47
Torquay United	46	13	8	25	42	68	47
Darlington	46	10	7	29	56	90	37

PROMOTION PLAY-OFFS

Stockport County 1   Stoke City 0
Peterborough United 2   Huddersfield Town 2

Stoke City.............................. 1   Stockport County 1
Stockport County win 2-1 on aggregate
Huddersfield Town.................. 1   Peterborough United..............2
Peterborough United win 4-3 on aggregate

Peterborough United 2   Stockport County 1

Promoted : - Brentford, Birmingham City & Peterborough United

Relegated : - Bury, Shrewsbury Town, Torquay United & Darlington

4th Division — Season 1991/92

	CREWE AL.	ROTHERM	MANSFIELD	BLACKPOOL	BURNLEY	SCUNTHORPE	SCARBORO'	NORTHAMPT.	DONCASTER	ROCHDALE	CARDIFF C.	LINCOLN C.	GILLINGHAM	WALSALL	HEREFORD	CHESTERFIELD	MAIDSTONE	CARLISLE U.	YORK CITY	HALIFAX T.	ALDERSHOT	WREXHAM	BARNET
CREWE ALEX.		0-1	1-2	1-0	1-0	1-1	3-3	1-1	1-0	1-1	1-1	1-0	2-1	0-1	4-2	3-1	1-1	2-1	1-0	3-2	4-0	2-1	3-0
ROTHERHAM U.	1-2		1-1	2-0	2-1	5-0	0-2	1-0	3-1	2-0	1-2	1-1	1-1	2-1	0-0	1-1	3-3	1-0	4-0	1-0	2-0	3-0	3-0
MANSFIELD T.	4-3	1-0		1-1	0-1	1-3	1-2	2-0	2-2	2-1	3-0	0-0	4-3	3-1	1-1	2-1	2-0	2-1	5-2	3-2	3-0	3-0	1-2
BLACKPOOL	0-2	3-0	2-1		5-2	2-1	1-1	1-0	1-0	3-0	1-1	3-0	2-0	2-0	3-1	1-1	1-0	3-1	3-0	1-0	4-0	4-2	
BURNLEY	1-1	1-2	3-2	1-1		1-1	1-1	5-0	2-1	0-1	3-1	1-0	4-1	2-0	2-0	3-0	2-1	2-0	3-1	1-0	2-0	1-2	3-0
SCUNTHORPE U.	1-0	1-0	1-4	2-1	2-2		1-1	3-0	3-2	6-2	1-0	0-2	2-0	1-1	1-1	2-0	2-0	4-0	1-0	1-0	1-0	3-1	1-1
SCARBOROUGH	2-1	0-3	0-0	1-2	3-1	4-1		2-1	1-0	3-2	2-2	1-1	2-1	2-3	1-1	3-2	2-0	2-2	1-0	3-0	0-2	4-1	0-4
NORTHAMPTON	0-1	1-2	1-2	1-1	1-2	0-1	3-2		3-1	2-2	0-0	1-0	0-0	0-1	0-1	1-1	1-0	2-2	2-2	4-0	1-0	1-1	1-1
DONCASTER R.	1-3	1-1	0-1	0-2	1-4	1-2	3-2	0-3		2-0	1-2	1-5	1-1	0-1	2-0	0-1	3-0	0-3	0-1	0-2	1-0	3-1	1-0
ROCHDALE	1-0	1-1	0-2	4-2	1-3	2-0	2-2	1-0	1-1		2-0	1-0	2-1	1-1	3-1	3-3	1-2	3-1	1-1	1-0	⊗	2-1	1-0
CARDIFF CITY	1-1	1-0	3-2	1-1	0-2	2-2	2-1	3-2	2-1	1-2		1-2	2-3	2-1	1-0	4-0	0-5	1-0	3-0	4-0	2-0	5-0	3-1
LINCOLN CITY	2-2	0-2	2-0	2-0	0-3	4-2	0-2	1-2	2-0	0-3	0-0		1-0	1-0	3-0	1-2	1-0	1-0	0-0	0-0	0-0	0-0	0-6
GILLINGHAM	0-1	5-1	2-0	3-2	3-0	4-0	2-0	3-1	2-1	0-0	0-0	1-3		4-0	2-1	0-1	1-1	1-2	1-1	2-0	3-1	2-1	3-3
WALSALL	2-3	0-2	3-3	4-2	2-2	2-1	0-0	1-2	1-3	1-3	0-0	0-0	0-1		3-0	2-2	1-1	0-0	1-1	3-0	3-1	0-0	2-0
HEREFORD U.	1-2	1-0	0-1	1-2	2-0	1-2	4-1	1-2	0-1	1-1	2-2	3-0	2-0	1-2		1-0	2-2	2-1	0-2	1-0	3-1	2-2	
CHESTERFIELD	2-1	1-1	0-2	1-1	0-2	0-1	1-0	1-2	0-0	2-2	1-5	3-3	0-1	2-0			3-0	0-0	1-3	4-0	2-1	1-1	3-2
MAIDSTONE U.	2-0	0-0	0-0	0-0	0-1	0-1	2-1	1-1	2-2	1-1	1-1	0-2	1-1	2-1	3-2	0-1		5-1	1-0	0-1	1-2	2-4	1-1
CARLISLE U.	2-1	1-3	1-2	1-2	1-1	1-0	0-0	2-2	2-1	3-3	1-0	1-2	3-0						1-1	1-1	⊗	0-1	1-3
YORK CITY	1-1	1-1	1-2	1-0	1-2	3-0	4-1	0-0	1-1	0-1	1-3	1-1	1-1	2-0	1-0	0-1	1-1	2-0		1-1	1-0	2-2	1-4
HALIFAX TOWN	2-1	0-4	1-3	1-2	0-2	1-4	1-0	0-1	0-0	1-1	1-1	1-4	0-3	1-0	0-2	2-0	1-1	3-2	0-0		⊗	4-3	3-1
ALDERSHOT	0-2	0-1	1-3	2-5	1-2	0-0	⊗	1-4	0-0	1-1	1-2	0-3	0-0	1-1	⊗	⊗	3-0	2-2	⊗	1-3		⊗	0-1
WREXHAM	1-0	0-3	3-2	1-1	2-6	4-0	2-0	2-2	1-2	2-1	0-3	1-1	2-1	2-1	0-1	0-1	0-0	3-0	2-1	2-0	0-0		1-0
BARNET	4-7	2-5	2-0	3-0	0-0	3-2	5-1	3-0	1-0	3-0	3-1	1-0	2-0	0-1	1-0	1-2	3-2	4-2	2-0	3-0	5-0	2-0	

	P	W	D	L	F	A	Pts
Burnley	42	25	8	9	79	43	83
Rotherham Utd	42	22	11	9	70	37	77
Mansfield Town	42	23	8	11	75	53	77
Blackpool	42	22	10	10	71	45	76
Scunthorpe Utd	42	21	9	12	64	59	72
Crewe Alex.	42	20	10	12	66	51	70
Barnet	42	21	6	15	81	61	69
Rochdale	42	18	13	11	57	53	67
Cardiff City	42	17	15	10	66	53	66
Lincoln City	42	17	11	14	50	44	62
Gillingham	42	15	12	15	63	53	57
Scarborough	42	15	12	15	64	68	57
Chesterfield	42	14	11	17	49	61	53
Wrexham	42	14	9	19	52	73	51
Walsall	42	12	13	17	48	58	49
Northampton Tn.	42	11	13	18	46	57	46
Hereford United	42	12	8	22	44	57	44
Maidstone Utd	42	8	18	16	45	56	42
York City	42	8	16	18	42	58	40
Halifax Town	42	10	8	24	34	75	38
Doncaster Rvrs	42	9	8	25	40	65	35
Carlisle United	42	7	13	22	41	67	34

⊗ Aldershot were declared bankrupt and obliged to resign from the league after playing 36 matches, results of which were declared void.

PROMOTION PLAY-OFFS

Barnet	1	Blackpool	0
Crewe Alexandra	2	Scunthorpe United	2

Blackpool	2	Barnet	0

Blackpool win 2-1 on aggregate

Scunthorpe United	2	Crewe Alexandra	0

Scunthorpe United win 4-3 on aggregate

Blackpool	1	Scunthorpe United	1 (aet)

Blackpool win 4-3 on penalties

Promoted : - Burnley, Rotherham United, Mansfield Town & Blackpool

(No Relegation)

72 St. Peters Avenue, Cleethorpes, DN35 8HU, England
24hr orderline (0472) 696226
Faxline (0472) 698546

VHS only

ALL PRICES INCLUDE POSTAGE

UK : 1st Class Letter Post

Overseas : Airmail Post

10% DISCOUNT
ON ALL ORDERS
IN EXCESS OF £60.00

UK - FORMAT VIDEOS (Suitable for UK, Europe & Australasia)

OFFICIAL HIGHLIGHTS OF THE SEASON

All priced :   £13.99 UK ;   £16.99 Overseas *(including postage)*

(All videos last 90 minutes unless shown otherwise)

1991/92

Arsenal	Aston Villa	Chelsea	Crystal Palace
Everton	Leeds United	Liverpool	Manchester City
Manchester United	Norwich	Nottingham Forest	Q.P.R.
Sheffield United	Sheff. Wednesday	Tottenham Hotspur	Ipswich Town
Leicester City	Middlesbrough	Millwall	Newcastle United
Swindon Town	Burnley are Back (60 mins)		Blackburn Rovers (60 mins)

1989/90 & 1990/91

Arsenal	Aston Villa	Chelsea	Crystal Palace
Everton	Leeds United	Liverpool	Manchester City
Manchester United	Nottingham Forest	Q.P.R.	Sheff. Wednesday
Tottenham Hotspur			

1988/89

Arsenal	Aston Villa	Chelsea	Everton
Liverpool	Manchester City	Manchester Utd.	Nottingham Forest
Tottenham Hotspur	Celtic (Scottish)		

Order From : **The Soccer Bookshelf (Dept SG9)**
72 St. Peters Avenue, Cleethorpes, DN35 8HU, England
Pay By : **Cash/Cheque/Postal Order or**
Credit Card : Access/Mastercard/Barclaycard/Visa/Amex

Other Supporters' Guides : -

THE SUPPORTERS' GUIDE TO NON-LEAGUE FOOTBALL CLUBS 1993

Featuring :
- all GM/Vauxhall Conference clubs
- all HFS Loans - Premier clubs
- all Beazer Homes - Premier clubs
- all Diadora Premier clubs
+ 180 other major Non-League clubs
112 pages - price £4.99 - post free

THE SUPPORTERS' GUIDE TO SCOTTISH FOOTBALL

Featuring :
- all Scottish League clubs
- all Highland League clubs
- all East of Scotland League clubs
+ Results, tables & full record of the Scottish National Team
96 pages - price £3.99 - post free